HOW TO GET THE MOST OUT OF

TRADE SHOWS

HOW TO
GET THE
MOST OUT OF
TRADE
SHOWS

Third Edition

STEVE MILLER

NTC Business Books
NTC/Contemporary Publishing Group

Library of Congress Cataloging-in-Publication Data

Miller, Steve (Steve A.), 1951–
     How to get the most out of trade shows / Steve Miller. —3rd ed., new and
rev. ed..
          p.   cm.
     Includes index.
     ISBN 0-8442-2347-6 (cloth)
     ISBN 0-658-00939-7 (paper)
     1. Trade shows.   2. Marketing.   I. Title.
     396.M55   1999
     659.1'52—dc21   98-46786
                                                                        CIP

Cover design by Scott Rattray
Interior design by JDA Typesetting

Published by NTC Business Books
A division of NTC/Contemporary Publishing Group, Inc.
4255 West Touhy Avenue, Lincolnwood (Chicago), Illinois 60712-1975 U.S.A.
Printed in the United States of America
International Standard Book Number: 0-8442-2347-6 (cloth)
                                                0-658-00939-7 (paper)
          03   04   05   LB   19   18   17   16   15   14   13   12   11   10   9   8   7   6   5   4   3

To Kay—my best friend, my partner, my love. I promised you it would never be dull. Was I right?

And to Kelly—my *big girl,* my joy, my light. I'll love you forever.

Contents

Foreword

Business has more marketing choices than ever. That's why it is essential to understand the fundamentals of effective strategic marketing. Exhibition organizers, exhibitors, and attendees must recognize the new marketing media available and integrate these alternatives in the exhibition marketing mix in order to remain competitive in today's global marketplace.

Over the past few years the exhibition industry has faced many new challenges as well as uncertainties in the economy and increased competition. Exhibition organizers and exhibitors must continually find ways to attract new customers as well as maintain relationships with existing customers while effectively utilizing financial and staff resources.

Exhibitions have been and will be the number one source for providing business opportunities between buyers and sellers. The real challenge is to maximize the effectiveness of exhibitions. That's where Steve Miller and his 16 years of international trade show experience can play a role. In his book Steve provides great insight into:

- Delivering measurable sales and marketing results
- Quantifying the return on investment (ROI)
- Delivering bottom line growth with increased revenue, reduced expenses, and higher margins

It is not unusual for exhibitors to lose focus on the fundamentals of effective exhibition marketing. Steve provides a comprehensive yet simple viewpoint for increasing business productivity and effectiveness. This revised edition of *How to Get the Most Out of Trade Shows* is a refreshing, easily understandable approach to accomplishing exhibition objectives. It's time to achieve greater results; and you can, by applying the concepts Steve outlines in this excellent book.

Patrick M. Cantini
Group Show Manager
Society of Manufacturing Engineers

Preface

I worked my first trade show 30 years ago. I hated it. I was surrounded by thousands of attendees, exhibit staffers, media, and guests—all of them strangers. I was way out of my comfort zone and needless to say, didn't do a good job of working the show. I developed a negative attitude about trade shows, which, happily for me, was shared by almost every other salesperson I met.

One day I was working a show, when an important customer stopped in. We chatted amiably for a few minutes, when she said, "You don't look very happy about being here."

I responded with the usual line. "Oh you know, trade shows are really a waste of time. We're only here because our competition is. And besides, if we didn't come, our absence would speak louder than our presence."

She poked me firmly in the chest. "Do you think I'm the only buyer walking through this show? Do you think that all those other buyers in the aisles aren't legitimate? And do you think that we don't have anything better to do than take a few days away from our office and waste time here at a trade show? If you're not getting any business from us, that's not our fault. That's yours!"

She was right, and it was a real wake-up call for me. I walked around the show and realized that most exhibit staffers had the same negative attitude I had. They didn't want to be there! Yet, as my visitor pointed out, there were thousands of potential customers walking through the aisles, looking for new suppliers. This was a huge, untapped opportunity.

I studied trade shows from all angles. I realized there was a lot more to exhibiting than just putting up a display, standing around, and waiting for something to happen (it usually didn't). I became good at trade show marketing and used that ability to help my companies more effectively and profitably exhibit at trade shows.

How to Get the Most Out of Trade Shows came as a result of a much-needed kick in the pants from a couple of close friends, Jim and Henriette Klauser. Without their persistence and encouragement, I don't think this book would ever have happened. Thanks, Jim and Henriette.

I would also like to thank those people who provided their valuable insight, support, and time in helping make this book possible: Bill Mee, Betsy Rogers, Gary Kerr, Phil Wexler, Jim Cathcart, George Walther, Melinda Lilley. A special note of thanks belongs to Herb Cartmell of American Image Displays for his input into show planning and booth design. And last, but certainly not least, my heartfelt thanks to Vanna Novak, Randi Freidig, and Marilyn Schoeman Dow; as the other three members of the Speakers4, they have been my biggest boosters and ego-builders.

Introduction

Trade shows may be the oldest form of marketing known to man. Yet despite their age, expositions are still one of the most powerful sales and marketing tools available to corporations today.

In the United States alone, there are thousands of trade shows and consumer shows. Some are small, local events lasting for just a few hours. Some are massive, mega-shows, involving thousands of exhibitors, investing millions of dollars to interact with attendees from around the world.

No matter what size the show, your objective as an exhibitor should always be the same—to measurably impact your overall corporate sales and marketing objectives. Unfortunately, the vast majority of exhibitors are unable to prove a quantifiable return-on-investment (ROI) on the major invested trade show dollars.

This book is written to help you overcome that obstacle.

Whether you are a new exhibitor or a veteran of hundreds of shows, it's important to understand that a well-run trade show is an investment in the future. And just like any well-managed investment, it provides a return based on initial objectives. This book will give you information on how to plan properly for that investment.

The first-time exhibitor will learn how to select the right trade shows, how to plan ahead, how to design a booth, how to attract prospects to the booth, how to sell on the floor, and how to follow up. It will give you solid information on how to assimilate successful trade shows into your current marketing mix.

For the veteran, this book provides a refresher course on the basics and covers some ideas and techniques that he or she might not know about. Although other trade show books concentrate on the exhibit planning area, this book focuses on the bottom line: active show promotion, training, prospecting, qualifying, floor selling, postshow follow-up, and evaluation.

Forms and checklists are included for all phases of trade show planning and implementation. Much of the information has been compiled through interviews with some of the top trade show marketers in various industries throughout the United States, as well as through discussions with top buyers. This book candidly gives you their impressions about trade shows, including the turnoffs and mistakes made by exhibitors. It'll show you how to attract top buyers to your booth and teach you how to sell to them.

The bottom line is simple: trade shows are hard work and expensive. *How to Get the Most Out of Trade Shows* will help you more efficiently prepare for that next show.

CHAPTER 1

The Scope of Trade Show Marketing

Imagine this: You're the head buyer for a large chain of consumer electronics stores, and your secretary buzzes you on the intercom. "Mr. Smith, a couple of reps from Worldwide Wonks are here to see you." You're busy, but decide to see them anyway.

As they enter, you notice they've brought a magician and two *Playboy* centerfolds with them. The models huddle around you, pose for a picture taken by one of the salesmen, stick a little fuzzy bird on the shoulder of your new Giorgio Armani suit, and hand you a plastic bag full of literature. The magician then begins his act—a rapid-fire display of card tricks accompanied by a running monologue telling you how the new Wonk will put magic into your sales. Meanwhile, the two salesmen find a couch in the corner of your office and light up a couple of smelly cigars. The magician continues his act while the models preen, smile, and sign glossy pictures of themselves for you to take home to your wife. Finally, the magician finishes his act.

One of the salesmen gets up, puts his arm around your shoulders, and confidently using his cigar as a pointer, gives you a pitch an old-time snake-oil salesman would be proud of. The other salesman grabs your phone, ignoring you. During the pitch, the first guy tries to demonstrate the new Wonk, but for some reason it won't work. He doesn't break stride. "It's a prototype," he explains, "but trust me, it's the finest Wonk ever engineered."

When you ask a question, the first salesman goes blank and looks to the second salesman, who merely shrugs his shoulders. "Gee, this is such a new

1

product, we'll have to call back to the home office to check on that," they chime. But they ask for the order anyway.

Sound familiar? Well, it may be a little far-fetched, but there is a point to all of this. If you wouldn't put up with this type of behavior as a buyer, why on earth would you consider it appropriate as a seller? Why is it that so many companies feel it's necessary to use this approach when marketing at trade shows?

Companies that use such Hollywood tactics to attract trade show buyers are missing the real purpose of the trade show medium. Granted, there is a big difference between making a field sales call and exhibiting your product to thousands of potential customers. But a trade show is a selling medium. Understanding the essential value of trade shows as a low-cost way of reaching new prospects, and knowing what financial effect they can have on your company's future, is imperative.

Why Trade Show Exhibitors Fail

As a consultant to the trade show industry, I feel like I've seen it all. Looking back to my first show as an exhibitor 30 years ago, I don't think exhibitors have changed much. Despite all the new information available to help corporations be better exhibitors, they still look and act much like they always did. And on top of it all, they still complain that trade shows don't provide any measurable return for their invested dollar.

This attitude continues to frustrate show managers. More and more trade and consumer expositions have attempted to educate their customers on all aspects of successful exhibiting, with mediocre success. Exhibitors want to complain about trade shows, but they don't want to do anything about it.

Why do corporations adopt this attitude of apathy and indifference? I think there are seven reasons why most exhibitors fail to use trade shows as effectively as they can.

1. *Trade shows are the most complicated form of marketing.* In reality, trade show marketing encompasses almost every other sales and marketing tool available. Direct mail, telemarketing, trade advertising, advertising specialties, billboards, TV, public relations, promotions, and literally a myriad of other marketing tools are all part of the trade show marketer's arsenal. A well-planned show considers all of these and develops a strategy that utilizes the best mix. Most corporations never take the time to study the different synergies that may be applied, and thus, never fully

utilize the unique potential of trade shows. At the American Health Care Association's annual show, DRIpride Corporation combined 11 different marketing tools to achieve stunning success. Within six months after the show, the company had generated a return of more than 15 times its trade show investment.

2. *Every show is different.* Every show has its own unique characteristics, determined by such factors as geography, total attendance, time of year, competition, state of the industry, total exhibitors, educational opportunities, *etc.* Yet most exhibitors approach every show, every year, in exactly the same way. For true success, corporations need to learn how to analyze a show's potential and then develop the best strategy for that show to achieve maximum success.

3. *Most corporations exhibit for wrong and/or unrealistic reasons.* How many corporations base their decision to exhibit on total attendance? They hear that 10,000 buyers will be at the show and think they're going to get a few thousand leads. Yet do they really have the plan in place or the ability to be able to qualify and follow up on that many? And how many companies go to trade shows simply for image because they feel their absence would speak louder than their presence? Trade shows are an extraordinary marketing tool when used properly and realistically. Unfortunately, most corporations don't understand that the real measure of a trade show's potential is its overall purchasing power and how much of that they can realistically expect to harvest. While several thousand attendees walked by, an exhibitor at WESTEC completely closed its booth for 50 invited visitors only. The company went after quality, not quantity.

4. *Most corporations don't know how to measure trade show success.* When it gets down to quantifying the return on their invested trade show dollars, most corporations are in the dark. As a result, when belts get tightened, trade shows are the first marketing tool to be cut back. Unless exhibitors know how to accurately forecast potential sales and put a plan in place for achieving those sales, the show doesn't get their marketing money. Throughout the short history of U.S. expositions, show after show has learned this lesson the hard way.

5. *Most staffers don't know why they are there or what to do.* It's common for exhibit staffers to receive little, if any, communication before a show. Too often it's limited to something like, "Here's your travel itinerary and booth schedule. See you there." Or, sometimes the company will have a preshow meeting, but it's usually for new product introduction and education. The fact is there are vast differences between working in the field and working a trade show, but most staffers have never been trained to

understand those differences and how to work a show. The exhibit staffer is the most important, yet most neglected, factor in achieving trade show success. For the reason why, see number 6.

6. *Exhibitors spend most of their time and money on the wrong side of the equation.* I look at the trade show equation as having two sides: hardware and software. Under the hardware column are such important factors as space rental, exhibit design and construction, shipping, drayage, I&D, show services, *etc.* Under the software column are such tools as direct mail, telemarketing, booth staffers, drawings, giveaways, postshow follow-up, *etc.* Which side will provide a company with the highest return on investment? The software side, of course. Yet, which side typically receives the vast majority of time, energy, and money? The hardware side, without a doubt. What's wrong with this picture? After U.S. Bank trained its exhibit staffers, more than $3 million in new loans were written from *one* show.

7. *Nobody taught them.* Ask exhibitors to think back to their first trade show and then ask a simple question: Who taught them how to work that show? The overwhelming answer is—no one. So how did they learn? Odds are they learned by watching and copying other exhibitors. As a result, exhibitors tend to look and act alike. Competition at trade shows doesn't breed creativity and innovation. It breeds conformity.

For years, show managers with good intentions have tried to educate their exhibitors through newsletters, mailings, and even seminars. Unfortunately, people don't read the mailings and don't attend seminars. Why? Because they think they already know what they're doing.

So where does that leave you? In a really great position. Trade shows can be your most powerful and most profitable marketing tool. And yet, most exhibitors fall down in maximizing their effectiveness. That leaves the door wide open for the company that is prepared to do trade shows right.

The rest of this book will show why your company should more aggressively approach your next trade show—and will show you how to do it profitably.

Why Trade Show Exhibitors Succeed
Cost-Effective Selling

The value of trade shows can be calculated using simple mathematics. Our own ongoing research of more than 70,000 corporate executives has shown that the average cost per sales call is in excess of $250. In addition, it takes an average of five to six sales calls to close an initial sale, making the average cost per sale in well over $1,250. Comparative research at exhibitions shows a similar cost per contact. However, the big difference is in the follow-up needed. Because of the exhibitor's ability to show three-dimensional products, offer hands-on demonstrations, and have immediate competitive comparison opportunity, the actual number of follow-ups after the show drops dramatically. In other words, the ultimate cost per sale is lower when initiated at a trade show.

Access to Potential Customers

We all know that salespeople are comfortable calling on clients they've been working with for years. They also like to believe that they know their territory better than anyone else. Maybe that's true. But do they know every potential customer? Do they really know every buyer at every company? It's doubtful. There are always new opportunities. The difficulty in making new contacts lies with a basic human condition: Everyone wants to be liked, and cold calling is tough on the ego. It's not fun; it's filled with rejection and is often demoralizing. It involves going to unfamiliar territory and calling strangers for appointments. And that's difficult. Getting to the right person is sometimes like picking your way through a funhouse filled with dead ends and deception. It is no wonder people don't like to venture outside their comfort zone.

Unfortunately, corporate growth requires new customers. Fortunately, trade shows represent one of the best and most cost-effective ways to obtain them. One of the beauties of trade shows is that buyers come to you. They schedule several days of their own time to travel to a show. They are off their turf. Buyers are there to look for new products for their own businesses. Believe it or not, if you have a product that fills a customer's needs, he or she wants to meet you. In fact, most established national shows draw thousands of potential new prospects.

According to a Trade Show Bureau report, at regional shows, fully 92 percent of the average exhibitor's visitors had not been called on by a salesperson during the previous year. According to Exhibit Surveys, Inc., over 90 percent of the average exhibitor's visitors have not been called on by a salesperson during the previous 12 months. So, if you see 200 legitimate buyers at a national show, 168 of them will be new contacts. How long would it take your sales force to come up with 168 legitimate new prospects?

Three-Dimensional Selling

If there's one advantage that trade shows have over newspapers, magazines, radio, outdoor billboards, television, and even field sales, it's this: At a trade show, you can set up your actual product to be displayed in its best light. Selling heavy equipment? Your prospect can climb all over that earthmover of yours and see live demonstrations of just how good it really is. Producing popcorn? A magazine ad doesn't compare to the actual aroma and taste of fresh-popped corn.

One-Stop Shopping

Gone shopping for shoes lately? Did you see a pair advertised in the paper and call the store to order them, or did you just buy the first pair in the first store you stopped at? Of course not. If you're an average shopper, you went down to the local mall. You tried on a few pairs at Steve's Shoes, then went to Shoes R Us to check out its selection. Then you strolled over to Shoe City and finally went to the If the Shoe Fits store. You compared styles, colors, and prices before you made your decision; and you were able to do it all in one convenient location—the mall.

That same advantage exists in trade shows; they resemble a temporary shopping mall. The presence of competitors encourages the buying process. Let's assume a prospect's interest is aroused by a particular type of product. If the interest is generated by a magazine ad, he or she must phone or write for more information. At a trade show, the prospect can come to your booth, see demonstrations, ask questions, then visit other manufacturers of similar products, each of whom offers a different selection of features. Such personal contact creates a sense of immediacy, and hence shortens the buying process.

Testing New Products

What better way to make a splash with a new product than premiering it at a trade show? Buyers are looking for new ideas, but at most shows they see last year's models with new colors. They tire of such routine displays—they want to see something new! This desire provides a great opening line to use on booth-browsers: "Have you seen our multilevel, variable speed, oscillating widget? It's new!" After they've stopped to see it, you can show them last year's models with new colors, too.

Trade shows also provide an immediate reading on the marketability of a new product. Do the buyers really like it? Is it priced too high or too low? Does it need a new design? Will they buy it? I used to take proto-types of products to shows to see how many actual orders I could get before I committed to manufacturing them. Instead of putting together an expensive market research project, hiring a focus group, and study-ing volumes of numbers, just take some samples to a big show. Top buyers are paid well to know whether a product will succeed or not. If it's a winner to buyers at a trade show, it's a good bet that it will be a winner in the marketplace.

The Growth of the Industry

Trade shows are big business. According to the Center for Exhibition Industry Research (CEIR), American industry invests more than $60 bil-lion a year in trade shows. Even more dramatic, the 1998 *Tradeshow Week Data Book* lists 4,295 shows in North America averaging 25,728 attendees visiting 325 exhibitors. That's more than 110 million attend-ees visiting 1.4 million exhibiting companies. More money is spent on trade shows than on magazine, radio, and outdoor advertising. Only newspapers and television receive substantially greater advertising funds.

Today's mega-extravaganza shows vary greatly from the bazaars of biblical times, which were originally set up where caravan routes crossed. For centuries the bazaar was the central focus for bartering and selling goods, services, information, even people.

The first real trade show was the 1851 World's Fair in London. Held for seven months in the temporary Crystal Palace, the fair showcased the achievements of the British Empire, then at its peak. The purpose of the World's Fair was to stimulate business for British companies in the international market. (Across the Atlantic in America, trade shows didn't really come into vogue until mass production was developed.)

Modern exhibitions, instead of focusing on general merchandise, have become specialized. If there's an industry or market for a product, it probably has a trade show. Health care, computer software and hard-ware, consumer electronics, advertising specialties, toys, and automo-biles are examples of industries that sponsor specialized trade shows.

As trade shows proliferate, so do the number of companies exhibit-ing and attendees registering. The exhibit arena has become tremen-dously competitive. Or has it? Although any good-size show certainly features many innovative displays and clever exhibiting strategies, a closer look reveals disappointing exhibitor behavior: backs turned while prospects examine products on display, eating and smoking while on duty, nonstop chatter with the pretty model as potential prospects stroll by, and ignoring customers while talking on the phone—to name but a few faults.

Also in evidence are the few exhibitors who take the show seriously. They know their products, warmly welcome prospects into their booths, aggressively qualify buyers, and appear alert to opportunity. These exhibitors have profitable shows.

Sponsoring a successful exhibit is a simple process. I'm not saying it's an easy process, just simple. Understanding the value of a trade show and recognizing its importance in your marketing plan will bring you a long way toward success.

Competitive Boost

Your company doesn't have the marketing budget of General Motors, Procter & Gamble, Sony, or Epson? Don't worry. Based on my own observations, a small business has an edge and sometimes a better marketing position at a trade show than a major company does. The reasons are simple. A typical national or international show usually features hundreds of exhibitors. Because the buyers can't see everyone, they must be selective. Yes, they will make a point of seeing the companies with 10,000-square-foot, three-story-high megabooths. But, because most shows are only open a total of 25 to 30 hours over a few days, most buyers will give an hour to one of these large exhibitors and its 200 SKU line, but that's about it. Buyers make time to walk the rest of the show, to see several small companies, because that's where they find the great new ideas. In fact, buyers often spend more time in small exhibits because they won't see them in the field; the big guys call on them every week.

To sum up, if you prepare properly, with aggressive preshow marketing, telemarketing, an attractive exhibit, good boothmanship, and a decent location, buyers will visit your exhibit.

CHAPTER 2

Planning the Show

Show Selection

Too many companies make the mistake of selecting a trade show merely because everyone else in the industry will be there. The smartest companies always thoroughly research a trade show before committing valuable time and money to attending it. They establish a set of criteria to evaluate a show's potential success in light of company plans. These criteria are also used to review previously attended shows. Times and trends change; a show that was perfect for the company five years ago may no longer have the same market. A critical review of any trade show is essential before any money is committed.

Before you can begin the search for the right show or shows, there are a number of questions you need to answer:

- What are our specific objectives at a trade show?
- Are we introducing a new product?
- Are we shining up the corporate image? If so, what image?
- Do we want to meet new prospects?
- Are we interested in direct sales?
- Do we want to build a mailing list?
- Will we get sales leads for our field salespeople?
- Are we researching the market for a new product or service?
- Will we sign up new distributors?
- Can success in achieving these goals be measured?

- Who is our target market?
- Which shows now attract our best customers?
- Which sales regions are the strongest?
- Will our distributors participate in our booth?
- Can we get co-op money for trade shows?
- Which shows conform to our budget timetable?
- Which shows conform to our manufacturing timetable?
- Which shows might aid problem sales areas?

The answers to these questions will determine the type of show your company should be using in its marketing mix and help you establish criteria for analyzing different shows.

Show Location

Once you've established your criteria, you need to compare all qualifying shows.

If you're in a specific industry with a fairly vertical market (for example, health care, consumer electronics, fishing, LAN), you can research available shows through several different sources. Contact any trade magazines in your field for a list of upcoming shows; they usually publish an annual issue containing a schedule of trade shows. Some even do it on an issue-by-issue basis.

Another way is to ask your competitors where they exhibit. You might be reluctant to do this, and sometimes they are reluctant to help, but the worst they can do is ignore your question.

Public libraries contain excellent business information resources. Most have directories of conventions and trade shows held around the world. Go to the business section and ask the reference librarians to help you find this information. The beauty of this system is that it's free!

Another good place to obtain information is in the *Tradeshow Week Data Book*. It provides information on trade and public shows held in the United States and Canada, provided the show's floor size exceeds 5,000 square feet. The only drawback is that the directory costs $349. (The address for *Tradeshow Week* is in the Appendix.)

If you're interested in shows in your region, contact your local convention center and visitors bureau. They usually have a list of all shows booked into your area, some several years in advance.

Show Analysis

When setting your objectives, you'll want to do a fairly complete analysis of the show, even if your company has been attending for years. Remember: times and trends change, and so do markets. The same trade show may no longer bring you the value for your dollar it once did.

Show Literature

The most obvious place to start the analysis is with the sales literature and information packet provided by the show management. It should tell you about the targeted attendees and any educational sessions scheduled; it usually contains a partial list of other exhibitors, too (including your competition). These packets cover a fairly broad spectrum of information in order to appeal to a wide range of possible exhibitors. For example, the Consumer Electronics Show product categories include car stereos, clocks, computers, nightclub equipment, health care electronics, telephones, and prerecorded videocassettes. Read these packets carefully. Are you positive this show is for you?

Show Management

Contact the show management for more information. Ask about the estimated audience size and profile. Do they have an attendee breakdown from the previous show? Get a list of last year's exhibitors. How many years has this show been going on? If it's fairly new, be careful. Ask about the management's background. Have they had successes with other shows? What type of advertising and promotion will they put on? Direct mail? Trade advertising? How much? How far in advance? Who is their target market? Is the show audited? How far in advance must you reserve a space? Most shows require a hefty deposit, so you might be tying up your money for a long period of time. Can exhibitors set up their own booths? What are normal working hours? What is overtime? What are the height and width of the entrances to the exhibit hall? Must hotel reservations be cleared through show management? Are there any restrictions on noise level, lights, entertainment? What insurance coverage does the show have?

The Competition and Other Exhibitors

How many companies have participated in the past? It's important to know whether the show is dominated by large or small space exhibitors. If there are mainly 60- to 80-foot booths and you have a tabletop display, you might get lost in the crowd. Conversely, if the show only has 10- and 20-foot spaces, and you're looking for a 2,500-square-foot island, you may be out of luck. As a general guideline for national shows, look for 30 percent of the space to be taken up by the megabooths, and the remaining 70 percent to be occupied by the 10- and 20-foot spaces. Such ratios make a good balance.

What do other companies think about the show? Call your competition. You're not asking them for their cost sheets or customer list, so don't worry. Usually people are happy to share insights into what they thought about a trade show. Ask them where they had problems (services? unions? low attendance? setting up?).

Geographics

Does your company have an adequate sales staff in the vicinity of the show? Even if it's a national show, most attendees will be from that region. If you don't have it well covered, you may be cutting out a large number of attendees as prospects.

Timing

Does the show conflict with any major holidays or events? I've seen trade shows held over the Fourth of July and during the Super Bowl. Neither was a good idea. What about your customers' timing? Do you have a particular selling season? If so, be sure the show is far enough in advance to accommodate the needs of the buyers as well as your production lines. Pay attention to buying trends, too. Years ago, for example, in the toy industry, orders were placed three to six months before Christmas shipping. Nowadays, buying plans are underway over a year ahead of time.

How does the timing fit in with your company's marketing plan? Does it fit well with new product introduction and production? Trade shows are traditionally a great place to bring out new products, but be sure to be true to your master plan.

Now that you've analyzed the show, you need to meld that information with your objectives. Ask yourself two questions: Based on my show analysis, will the company be able to reach its objectives? If the show analysis does not meet corporate objectives, should we go? This doesn't need to be a black-and-white issue. Sometimes the answer lies in how much you decide to participate. Maybe a smaller booth would prove more appropriate. Maybe the company could spend less on advertising and promotion. Perhaps you don't even need to exhibit and can accomplish some objectives by just attending or having a hospitality suite.

By using these sources, you should be able to glean enough show information to decide which shows are most advantageous for your company's exhibitions.

Preshow Planning

After you've selected the right show for your company, the real work begins. To ensure success at a trade show, it's important to put together a detailed plan of action. What's the big deal? Once you've selected the show, the steps are simple, right? All you have to do is get a booth, choose a booth location, pack up some products, and go. After all, isn't that the way most companies do it?

Well, yes, that is the way most companies prepare for trade shows; that's also why most companies are wasting their marketing resources. They might as well just stand on a street corner and hand out $50 bills.

A well-planned trade show will make you and your company successful trade show marketers. Smart companies use trade shows as an integral and effective part of their marketing mix. They know that the planning process will make or break the success of that particular show.

Unlike many projects a company undertakes, a trade show has one big advantage—a deadline. You know the date of the exhibition and can work backward from it. There should be several parts to your plan:

- Show objectives
- Preshow analysis
- Budget planning
- Target market identification
- Choosing display products
- Advertising and promotion plans
- Coordination of company personnel
- Determination of show staff and size (Do you plan to train them?)
- Staff responsibilities

- Lead generation and conversion
- Postshow follow-up: alternatives and timeline for preparation

Setting Your Goals

In the past, corporations used exhibitions and conventions as dog and pony shows. They displayed products, put on a few demonstrations, and did a lot of wining and dining. They never sold anything at the show; instead, they used it to create goodwill with customers and prospects. Unfortunately, most companies still believe that trade shows function in this manner. They don't set measurable objectives and, consequently, have no way of judging how successful a show is.

Companies still justify their corporate presence at trade shows with nebulous reasons. I'm frequently told by representatives of corporations that they attend trade shows merely because it enhances the company's image; it's good for PR; it supports the association and the industry; and it's necessary to maintain face with competitors. What a waste of corporate time and money. Such attitudes are old-fashioned; don't get caught up in them. If your advertising agency came to you and suggested running an expensive direct mail campaign to your target market for no particular reason, with no specific and measurable goals in mind, would you do it? Chances are you'd start looking for a new ad agency.

Corporations for years have said they can't project success through trade shows. Let's think about that. Every fiscal new year, your company projects next year's numbers, right? Where do those numbers come from? Odds are upper management just took last year's figures and added 8 percent. Or you've had several years of experience and can use trends and intelligent projections. If you can do it for an entire year, surely you can do it for three or four days.

In contrast, attendees go to trade shows to find solutions to company problems, to compare vendors, to finalize purchase selections, to discover new methods and developments in the industry, and to meet with technical experts. Attendees at trade shows have learned that they need to be fiscally responsible. Anytime they spend money, they must justify it. In fact, my experience has been that attendees take the shows more seriously than the exhibitors. For example, I've been working with the Food Marketing Institute for several years, putting on trade show marketing seminars regionally and "boothmanship" seminars on-site immediately before the show. We have never had more than 150 exhibitors attend any of these sessions. We started putting on a "How to Get the Most Out of the Convention" seminar for the attendees and now have more than 1,000 participants each year! Exhibitors need to be just as careful about supporting any expenditures. A successful trade show marketer ties in corporate objectives with the attendees' to attain specific, measurable goals and objectives.

When you set your goals, be sure to make them quantifiable by asking such questions as who? how many? and how much? Following are some objectives you might want to consider.

Forecast Sales

Actual sales (dollars or quantity) can be based on total on-site sales, average sales per customer, sales to existing customers, sales to new customers, sales per product, and sales achieved over a specified period of time following the show. It is important to be realistic about your projections—don't just pick numbers out of a hat. For example, if you expect to write orders with your current customers, write down the names of those you expect to see at the show. Project what percentage of them will write orders. Fix an average dollar amount per order and multiply that by the number of orders for your total sales goal.

Project Lead Generation

Again, the important thing is to be realistic. If you only have two people at a time working a show that's open for a total of 22 hours, don't expect 1,000 leads, even if there are 100,000 attendees. It's just not going to happen. As a rule of thumb, figure that each salesperson will average six contacts per hour. The earlier example of two people working a booth for 22 hours brings the following results:

2 salespeople × 6 contacts/hour = 12 total contacts/hour

12 contacts/hour × 22 hours = 264 show contacts

This figure, of course, is only an estimate. Some products are conducive to higher contacts per hour and others to lower. In addition, current customers are included in the contacts per hour.

Thus, using the above example, for every 22 current customers you see, you will see one less new prospect per hour. Keep in mind that this figure represents total contacts, not qualified prospects.

Miller's Formula

Here's a formula I developed several years ago that can help you define your goals:

	1. Total show hours
×	2. Total staffers during each hour
=	3. Total staff/hours
×	4. Number of contacts/hour
=	5. Total show contacts
×	6. % of attendees fitting your target market
=	7. Total number of targets reached
×	8. Closing %
=	9. Total number of sales (by when?)
×	10. Average sale
=	11. Total sales
×	12. Length of relationship
=	13. Long-term ROI

Let's walk through an example. Say the show is open for 20 hours total (1) and you have four staffers working each hour (2). That gives you a total of 80 staff-hours during the show (3). Your staffers average talking with 15 people per hour (4), which means they'll talk with a total of 1,200 attendees (5). According to your research, approximately 16 percent of the attendees fit your target market (6). That means that after greeting and qualifying 1,200 attendees, your staffers will uncover 192 people who fit your target market (7). You know from experience that your staffers close approximately 20 percent of their prospects (8), which yields roughly 38 sales (9) in six months. Your average sale is $5,000 (10), providing you with $190,000 in revenues (11). Your average customer stays with your company for four years (12), which gives you long-term revenues of $760,000.

You can use this formula to project figures for an upcoming show, based on whatever specific objectives you have. If your objective is on-site sales, then your objective is number 9—38 sales. If your objective is generating leads, then you're looking at number 7—192 leads.

Enhancing Relationships

As I said earlier, I believe the purpose of business is to create and maintain long-term relationships. Too often, corporations go to trade shows focused on simply *creating* new relationships and ignoring the maintenance. Trade shows offer a fantastic opportunity to reinforce and enhance your current customers' intelligent decision to work with you. After all, you can present focused, customized presentations, based on your intimate knowledge of their company, and this gives them the opportunity to immediately comparison-shop you against your competition.

With the exception of brand new companies, or companies breaking into a new market, you need to set up a combination goal, including both new prospects and current customers.

Additional Considerations

Keep in mind the following additional benefits afforded by trade show participation.

- A trade show is a good place to introduce a current product to a new market or industry. New leads and sales are strong possibilities. Introducing a new product, service, or a new feature on an established product is also a good idea at a trade show.
- Product and company image can be promoted among attendees, in the industry, and in the show's geographic vicinity. Awards and media coverage are two ways to meet these objectives.
- Learn more about your competition and industry trends. Knowing what's new, who's hot, and what the most talked-about product at the show is can broaden your product knowledge, making you a stronger competitor in the industry.

- Trade shows allow you to conduct market research on new products. Feedback on a product's color, price, appeal, and value can be gathered. Market research among attendees can also reveal open niches. Needs that aren't being met require solutions.
- Give customers a rare opportunity to meet with your corporate bigwigs and technical support staff. Often these are people your customers never meet. The connection with your customers can be strengthened by this contact.
- Position the trade show *within* your overall marketing plan. Don't make the mistake of isolating it. Your company has corporate objectives; tie the trade show in with them. Develop a synergistic relationship between trade shows, direct marketing, corporate public relations, advertising, and all other parts of the marketing mix.

Setting Your Budget

Once you've made the decision to go to a show, the next step is to create a budget. This is a fairly simple, yet necessary, part of trade show planning. The amount of money you allocate depends largely on your objectives and how they tie in with what the show can potentially produce. There are seven basic categories in the budget: space rental, the exhibit, shipping and storing, show services, personnel, advertising and promotion, and travel and entertainment. When you first start planning for the show, estimate your budget using these seven categories. (See Figure 2-1.)

Figure 2-1 Estimated Exhibit Budget Form

Budget	Estimate	Actual
1. Space Rental	_____	_____
2. Exhibit Expenses	_____	_____
3. Shipping and Storing	_____	_____
4. Show Services	_____	_____
5. Personnel	_____	_____
6. Advertising and Promotion	_____	_____
7. Travel and Entertainment	_____	_____
Total	_____	_____

If you have past trade show records, use them to determine most of the numbers; just remember, this is an estimate only, not a strict guideline. If you break down each part of the budget into more detail, expenses can be more easily determined.

Space Rental

Most companies don't spend any time determining how much booth space to rent. New exhibitors and small companies automatically send in for 10-foot (linear) booth spaces and then plan from there. Practically, the amount of space you rent should be directly related to your show objectives and how many people will be working the booth.

For example, you are attending a show that will be open 24 hours. Information research indicates there will be 80 current customers at the show; you set a goal of seeing 75 percent of them. You have also set an objective of generating 300 new, qualified leads. Thus, the total numbers of customers and contacts you intend to see comes to 360.

Of course, there will be a certain percentage of attendees who come into your booth who won't be qualified buyers. They might have a specific need that your product line doesn't fill. They might be trade show press (yes, they are important, but they aren't qualified leads). They might just be old buddies who stop by to talk about old times. They might be "lookie-loos"—the people who don't belong in the show but come anyway. A lookie-loo could be a local just out for a day of entertainment or a spouse of someone working the show. It's important for you to weed these people out as quickly as possible to avoid wasting valuable time. Remember, at a trade show, you only have a finite number of minutes to put to profitable use; don't waste them on these people.

After you've spent a couple of minutes with an attendee, ask yourself this question: Is the time I'm spending right now moving me closer to my show objectives? If the answer is no, quickly move the conversation to a close. Don't worry about seemingly rude behavior. Most legitimate buyers will want to move on to exhibits that most interest them, too. Politely say, "I can tell by our conversation that we don't have the product/service you're looking for. I don't want to waste any more of your time because I know there are many other exhibitors you want to see. Thank you for stopping by."

There's a wonderful little time-management tool available at any local office supply store that you can give each of your staffers. It's a ¼-inch round, color-coding label. A box of these costs only a couple of bucks and can help keep your staffers on track throughout the show.

Give each of your staffers one of these and tell them to put one on the face of their watch, right smack in the middle. They look at their watches more during a trade show than in any other situation. The label "Geez, have I only been here an hour?" (I prefer green—it represents money to me) jumps out and reminds them to ask themselves: Is what I'm doing right now moving me closer to or further away from my objectives? If they're in some time-wasting activity, they'll be reminded to get back in gear.

No matter how quickly you get rid of an unqualified prospect, however, he or she will still take up some of your time. For example, if, during a 22-hour trade show, you spend two minutes apiece with three unqualified attendees per hour, you've lost 132 minutes—more than two hours of your time!

Because of these unqualified attendees, there is an R-factor you need to consider; the R stands for "Reject." A certain percentage of the people you meet will automatically be rejected in the qualifying process. Therefore, the next question to ask is: What percentage of people coming into the booth will be rejects? Unless you have accurate figures from past shows, this figure will be tough to project. Several large companies have informally researched this factor, and the percentages range from 16 to 50 percent. Knowing what percentage of the attendees will be interested in your product helps determine the percentage. If you're exhibiting gourmet candy at a specialty food show, interest will be much higher than if you exhibit at a gift show. A good reject figure to start with is 25 percent; adjust the percentage based on your knowledge of the show audience.

Let's go back to the earlier example and plug in the 25 percent R-factor. The goal is to make 360 qualified contacts at the show. Sixty of these are current customers, so 300 new contacts must be made. If 25 percent of the contacts will be rejected, then 75 percent must be qualified. The calculations would be:

Total contacts × 75% = 300 qualified contacts
Total contacts = 400

Adding the 60 current customers to this number brings the required number of attendees to 460. This figure helps determine the number of people needed to work the booth and how much booth space you need.

You've already determined that you need to make 460 contacts in 22 hours. That's an average of 21 contacts per hour. If you figure that one salesperson makes six contacts per hour, then you need four people in the booth at all times (21 divided by 6 = 3.5). Round that number up to four, or if you have to, down to three.

Plan on more than one shift for your salespeople. After a couple of hours working a show, a salesperson begins to become ineffective. In this example, you'd need eight salespeople for the two shifts.

Research has established that each salesperson on duty needs approximately 50 square feet of unoccupied space to work in. In addition, the exhibitor must determine the amount of space to be occupied by the booth itself, products, tables, and chairs; figure another 50 percent of that space for such things. So, for every salesperson on duty, you need 75 square feet of booth space. Four salespeople require 300 square feet. This is the approximate figure for a salesperson plus an attendee. Calculations are shown in the section on "Booth Dimensions" in Chapter 3.

Once you've determined the number of people you need and the space required to accommodate them, you can project how much to budget for space rental.

Let's be frank, though. These calculations are designed to reflect ideal situations. Not all of us can afford a 300-square-foot exhibit. However, these formulas do provide a checks-and-balances system for your objectives. Are you projecting to get 300 new contacts, when you can only budget for a 100-square-foot booth? Maybe you should reevaluate your goals to avoid being disappointed by the postshow results.

Don't be discouraged if you can only project 120 new leads at a show. What percentage of those leads will you be able to close? If you were only able to get 10 new customers, how much will they be worth to you over the next 10 years? Be realistic about your objectives, but also recognize that trade shows can be very cost-effective.

Exhibit Expenses

Many questions arise here. Do you even *have* an exhibit? How old is it? Is it big enough to handle your space requirements? How much refurbishing does it need? Do the design and colors still fit within the corporate image and your objectives? Is it custom-made or portable? Which do you need now? (I'll get into more detail about the actual design and construction of booths in Chapter 3. Here, we are examining the budget requirements only.) Six areas need to be addressed.

Design and construction.   Before we discuss the hows and whats of design and construction, let's first talk about the why. Why do you need an exhibit? What is its purpose?

You'll hear many people, especially designers, tell you that the exhibit is an extension of your company. It symbolically represents who you are to the industry, and therefore needs to be designed with that in mind. They'll also tell you the exhibit is your staffers' home-away-from-home, where they will represent your company and present your products or services. I'll grant you the booth does represent your company and does support your staffers, but neither of those is its *primary* purpose.

The primary purpose of your exhibit is simple:

It gets your targeted market to *stop*.

Remember, if the booth brings *everybody* in, you have a big job of culling the qualified traffic from the nonqualified. If it tries to be all things to all people, it isn't anything to the right people. And if your targeted attendee doesn't stop, you have no show.

So keep in mind the primary purpose of your exhibit when sitting down with your exhibit house and/or designer.

Do you require a custom booth? If so, you'll need to have it designed. There are two ways to do this, each having a different impact on your budget.

You can hire an exhibit design specialist. This is expensive, but if your budget allows, a custom-designed booth will help you more easily reach your goals. The specialist should design your booth for easy shipping, long life, and ease in setup. Exhibit Surveys, under the commission of the Trade Show Bureau, determined that a new custom construction costs an average of $801 per linear foot for a back-walled display and $41 per square foot for an island or peninsula display.[1]

The best way to find a good designer or exhibit house is to ask other exhibitors. When you're at a show, look for well-designed booths, and then ask for the names of the designers. If you can't find one that way, look in the Yellow Pages or contact the Exhibit Designers and Producers Association for a list of members:

Exhibit Designers and Producers Association
611 E. Wells Street
Milwaukee, WI 53202
414/276-3372

[1]These figures are from the "Trade Show Bureau's Research Report No. 2060," November 1988.

If you have designers on staff capable of designing and constructing a booth to fit your requirements, great. But be careful that they do, in fact, know what they're doing. Designing an easy-to-build, easy-to-ship, and easy-to-take-down booth is no simple feat. If you're doing it in-house just to save money, you're doing it for the wrong reason.

Graphics. If you're designing or buying a new exhibit, it will come with new graphics; if you're not, make sure your graphics are up-to-date. Although it's not cheap to update your graphics regularly for each show, it's necessary. Ask your designer for an estimate.

Refurbishing. Trade shows are hard on exhibits. During setup, tear-down, and shipping, exhibits get banged around. No matter how sturdy they are, they take a beating and eventually show it. You should plan to refurbish your exhibit annually. Remember, your exhibit is your showcase. The first thing people see when walking down an aisle is the exhibit. If it's in bad shape—dirty, worn out, broken at the edges, partially lit from broken light fixtures—that is the impression your current and future customers will have of your company. Contact your exhibit house for the costs to refurbish.

Products for display. Your company may build the products for display, but you've still got to pay for them. Put it in your budget.

Booth rental. You might not want to buy an exhibit. Maybe you don't know if you want to commit to trade shows long term, or perhaps your company has committed its only booth to another show. The good news on renting is you don't worry about shipping, setting up, tearing down, or storage costs. The bad news is that rental exhibits are boring and will not stand out at a busy show.

Used booths. Companies are always trading in or selling their old booths when designing new ones. Sometimes you can find a well-designed exhibit that is functional for your use and reasonably priced. Be prepared to spend some money on refurbishing, and make sure it's strong enough to display your products!

Keep in mind the projected life span of your booth. If you use it for more than one show (which I hope you do), amortize the cost over all the applicable shows. For example, if you invest $10,000 in a new booth and plan to use it in five different shows, put down $2,000 as the cost of the booth on your budget.

Shipping

I won't go into a complete discussion on transportation, but here is a brief overview. Most exhibits are shipped one of three ways: common carrier, van line, and air freight. Each has its advantages and disadvantages.

Common carrier. The biggest advantage for a common carrier is it's usually the cheapest way to go. The major disadvantage is that the common carrier is not designed to carry trade show exhibits, but merely to transport freight. Scheduling is also not exact; allow more time to get to the show. If you know how many cubic feet the exhibit covers and its weight, you can get quotes by phone.

Van line.   Most of us relate van lines to moving household goods; however, most large van line companies have special departments for handling trade show exhibits. They understand your needs and will work closely with you. The disadvantage is cost, although deregulation has brought costs down somewhat. In the long run, this is the best shipping choice. They will provide rough quotes by phone, just as common carriers do.

Air carrier.   If it absolutely, positively has to be there overnight—or if your company is having a contest to see who can foolishly spend the most money—use an air carrier. Otherwise, don't.

Show Services

Whether you like it or not, odds are you'll have to hire some type of service, and if you use any services at trade shows, you will have to work with unions.

If you need labor for setting up your exhibit, get an independent contractor to hire workers and supervise setup. You'll be provided a supervisor with whom you can work and you'll probably get a prescreened group from the labor pool. This type of organization will give you higher quality performance and fewer problems. Be sure and arrange this help well in advance of the show and also provide the show organizer with written notification that you will be working with an independent and authorized labor source.

Pay attention to how you schedule labor. Overtime begins after a certain hour during weekdays and is in effect all weekend. Labor is expensive and does not charge by fractions of the hour. Labor contracts usually provide for a two-man crew with a minimum charge of one hour per man. Costs add up quickly; if you can set up during a weekday, you'll save money.

If you don't want to work with an independent contractor, it's doubly important to arrange labor in advance. If you wait until you get to the show, you might be stuck with fill-in labor, since all the professional labor has been preassigned. Many people suspect that theft and attitude problems come mainly from fill-ins.

Be careful to coordinate the job assignment for booth setup with the delivery of your exhibit. It's a common sight at a show to see labor sitting around an empty booth waiting for the exhibit to arrive. Don't worry, though; they're patient about waiting. After all, even if they're not working you're still paying them—a lot.

If things don't go exactly as you plan, be patient and try to work things out. If there's a major problem with labor, go to the official Service Contractor and discuss it with them. Don't ask for trouble by getting upset; you're on their turf.

Of course, if you've got a custom display, you don't have any choice. You'll be using union help to put it up. But if you have a small portable exhibit, how do you get around having to hire expensive union help?

Technically, you probably can't. But there is an unwritten rule that usually applies. It's called the Half-Hour Rule. What this means is that if you can hand-carry your exhibit into the exhibition hall, and set it up by yourself in less than 30 minutes, the unions usually won't bother you. I say usually because I've been in certain convention centers (that shall remain nameless to protect my future participation) where the unions wouldn't even let me put up a tabletop display. Fortunately, most halls aren't like that. Most union workers are hardworking, conscientious people who want to do a good job, given a chance.

Besides using labor for helping in the booth setup and breakdown, there are a number of other services available—electrical, furniture rental, telephone, carpeting, signage, cleaning, security, computer rental, and photographer. Again, contract as far in advance as is possible for any services you require.

A word about security. Don't ever assume your products are safe. If there's any doubt, hire some security. If your products are small enough to fit in a security cage, rent one. If not, get a guard. True, it's another expense, but it's a lot less expensive to hire a security guard than to be at a show with little or nothing to exhibit.

There is the classic story of the exhibitor who didn't hire a security guard for his expensive consumer electronics. The reason? The large exhibit across the aisle from him had several guards watching the display, so he assumed they'd keep an eye on his. The next morning he arrived to an empty booth. All his products had been stolen. And the security guards in his neighbor's booth claimed they didn't see a thing.

Personnel

Several years ago, the company I worked for contracted for a 30-foot by 30-foot island space in the Premium/Incentive Show in New York. In addition, we invested about $60,000 in a new booth to dazzle our prospects.

As it turned out, the booth never made it to New York. About an hour before the show opened, I was standing in the middle of a 900-square-foot area of concrete with 15 of my salespeople. I looked at the group and asked, "What do we do now?" One of the staffers looked at me with despair and said, "I guess this means we have to work!"

We had our best show ever.

The fact is, your staffers are *the* most important tool in your trade show arsenal. If you don't believe me, leave all your staffers home for your next show and see what kind of results you get from your display and all the rest of the hardware.

Not all companies put personnel as a category in their budget. I believe it's important, even though it is actually an indirect cost. It doesn't directly come out of your show budget, but it does cost your company to have those people there.

Training

Remember the hardware versus software discussion? Don't make the mistake of ignoring your most important tool—your staffers. Do they *really* know how to work a show? Do they *really* understand the difference between working out in the field and working at a trade show? Do they *really* know why they are there and what they are expected to accomplish? Do they *really* know how to approach a total stranger in a foreign environment, qualify that person, uncover their need, present your product/service, set up the close, and disengage?

A company in Seattle that had just purchased a $150,000 display contacted me about training its 25 staffers. After some discussion, I quoted the investment the company would be making in my participation. They gasped at the figure. "But we only have $500 in our training budget!"

What's wrong with this picture?

Your staffers will make or break your show. Before you invest in anything else, invest in them.

Wages/Salaries

Estimate the cost of each salesperson's time to your company. If you want to be really accurate, include *all* compensation—salary, commission, bonus, and benefits. Total this up for a year and divide by 230 (the average number of workdays after subtracting vacation, holidays, and some sick days). This gives you the average cost per day for that person.

For example, Scott M. makes $30,000 base pay, plus another $10,000 in commissions and bonuses annually. His benefits (health insurance and company car) total another $7,500. His total compensation package is $47,500 per year. Divide that $47,500 by 230, and Scott costs approximately $207 per day. If Scott spends five days at the trade show, his total cost is $1,035.

Do this simple calculation for each person going to the show to obtain the total personnel time figure. If you don't know or can't get exact compensation figures, estimate salary and benefits. The important thing is to have something down in this category.

Outside help.   Sometimes you need extra people. Whether it's a magician, an actor, or someone hired to demonstrate your products, be sure and project the cost into your budget.

Advertising and Promotion

As I said at the beginning of this chapter, the average exhibitor rents booth space, puts up the booth, hangs a sign, and then waits around for the buyers to flock in. That's the way we'd all like it to happen, but it doesn't.

The few days that the trade show is open represent only one-third of the total trade show marketing process. The other two-thirds are preshow planning and postshow follow-up. The entire marketing event, if done correctly, takes several months.

Advertising and promotion are an integral part of the total picture. In a study conducted for the Trade Show Bureau (now the Center for Exhibition Industry Research), Robert T. Wheeler, Jr., identified eight factors influencing attendees' decisions to visit specific exhibits.

1. Obligation: 25 percent. Based on past business activities or relationships, attendees feel an obligation to visit.
2. Habit: 23 percent. The attendee has been visiting a particular exhibit for several years, and as long as the exhibitor is there, he or she will stop by.

3. Personal invitation: 15 percent. When a targeted prospect received a personal invitation from a sales or corporate representative, he or she made a point to visit.
4. Trade journal publicity: 12 percent. Make sure to get as many news and feature stories in trade journals as possible.
5. Advertising: 9 percent. Advertise your products and show location in preshow issues of the trade journal.
6. Mail invitations: 9 percent. Although not as effective as personal invitations, they still bring a good response. Send information and invitations to as many qualified prospects as possible.
7. Recommendations from associates: 3 percent. You can have an effect on this factor.
8. Not sure: 3 percent. These people are undecided.[2]

In my opinion, exhibitors have a lot of control over numbers 3, 4, 5, and 6, and partial control over number 7; that's control of 49 percent of all reasons attendees visit a selected exhibit.

Also include in your budget any on-site handouts, giveaways, press kits, or anything else that falls under this category. I'll discuss all advertising and promotion in more detail in Chapter 4.

Travel and Entertainment

Like the personnel category, most companies don't figure the cost of travel and entertainment into their show budget. But it's still there.

Ask your travel agent for the airline and hotel figures. Then estimate how much entertainment (do you have a hospitality suite?) you need to include.

Finalizing Your Budget

Once you've figured numbers for each of the seven areas of your budget, it's time to put it all together. Use Figure 2-2 as a guideline for developing your own customized budget.

---

[2]These figures came from Robert T. Wheeler, Jr.'s survey in the "Trade Show Bureau Research Report No. 13," July 1982.

Targeting Your Market

As I have stated, I believe the purpose of business is to create and maintain long-term relationships. In today's marketplace, if you don't know who, what, and where your true prospects are, or if you fail to communicate with them as individuals, you will lose ground to competitors who do.

The thing to keep in mind is that, with few exceptions, not every attendee at a trade show is a potential prospect. Most shows just aren't designed that way. In fact, according to a Center for Exhibition Industry Research report, approximately 16 percent of all attendees at an average show will be qualified prospects.[3]

As mentioned earlier, people attend trade shows to look for solutions to specific problems, finalize selections for purchase after the show, identify any new methods or developments in their field, and meet with technical experts. Each of these reasons is personal to each prospective buyer. Therefore, there is no such thing as a universal product, that is, one for which every attendee is a buyer.

Do you already know who your target market is? Great! Then all you have to do is define those customers or clients so that your show staff will also be able to identify them.

Profiling Your Ideal Customer

If individuals make up your target market, consider the following questions:

- Are they male, female, or both?
- Are they married, single, or divorced?
- How old are they?
- What is their net worth?
- Where do they live?
- How much do they travel?
- How much education do they have?
- What are their favorite sports?
- How many kids do they have?
- Do they own computers?

[3]This figure came from Exhibit Surveys, Inc., Red Bank, New Jersey.

Figure 2-2 Customized Exhibit Budget Form

Name of Show _____

Date of Show _____

Exhibit Budget

Item	Budget	Actual
1. Space Rental	_____	_____
2. Exhibit Expenses	_____	_____
a. Design and construction	_____	_____
b. Graphics	_____	_____
c. Refurbishing	_____	_____
d. Products for display	_____	_____
e. Booth rental	_____	_____
f. Used booth purchase	_____	_____
g. Total exhibit expenses	_____	_____
3. Shipping and Storage	_____	_____
a. Freight	_____	_____
b. Drayage	_____	_____
c. Exhibit storage	_____	_____
d. Total shipping and storage	_____	_____
4. Show Services	_____	_____
a. On-site labor (setup)	_____	_____
b. On-site labor (teardown)	_____	_____
c. Electrical	_____	_____
d. Furniture rentals	_____	_____
e. Misc. rentals (plants, etc.)	_____	_____
f. Telephone	_____	_____
g. Carpeting	_____	_____
h. Signage	_____	_____
i. Cleaning	_____	_____

j. Security _____ _____

k. Computer rental _____ _____

l. Photography _____ _____

m. Imprinter rental _____ _____

n. Florist _____ _____

o. Audiovisual equipment _____ _____

p. Other _____ _____

q. Total show services _____ _____

5. Personnel _____ _____

   a. Wages/salary _____ _____

   b. Outside help _____ _____

   c. Training _____ _____

   d. Total personnel _____ _____

6. Advertising and Promotion _____ _____

   a. Preshow advertising and
      promotion _____ _____

   b. On-site advertising and
      promotion _____ _____

   c. Postshow advertising and
      promotion _____ _____

   d. Total advertising and promotion _____ _____

7. Travel and Entertainment _____ _____

   a. Airfare _____ _____

   b. Housing _____ _____

   c. Staff meals _____ _____

   d. Client meals and entertainment _____ _____

   e. Hospitality suite _____ _____

   f. Miscellaneous _____ _____

   g. Total travel and entertainment _____ _____

Total Show Expenses _____ _____

If your target market is a business, consider these questions:

- What is its sales volume?
- How many employees?
- What industry is it in?
- What type of phone system does it use?
- How are customers reached? Direct sales? Telemarketing? Direct mail?
- Does it have a fleet of cars? Are they leased?
- Is it in mail order?
- Does it use advertising specialties?

You'll want to break down responses to these questions into four areas of criteria:

- How do you define decision makers, influencers, or specifiers? What is their title or area of responsibility? Be aware of Vertical Buying Teams (VBTS), made up of a combination of all these important people. You might be talking with the specifier one day, and the others the next day for more detailed discussion.
- What need must they have that your product or service fills?
- Will they be able to afford your product or service?
- When will they be in the market to buy?

The questions in these lists are by no means complete; they represent only a sample of the type of questions you should ask about your target market. The idea is to stimulate you to ask detailed questions in order to identify your ideal client or customer. Once you are able to do this, you are in a better position to find your prospects at the trade show and attract them into your booth.

Trade Show Countdown

The Japanese taught the Americans a valuable way to handle inventory. It's called "Just-in-Time." The whole idea is that production parts are not brought into the factory until the assembly line needs them. This practice saves on space and on the cost of keeping a large inventory of spare parts. Just-in-Time is a wonderful method, requiring a tremendous amount of coordination with suppliers to provide the products when they are needed. Unfortunately, Just-in-Time preparation is a common practice among trade show exhibitors, although it is not usually intentional.

The typical scenario occurs about four weeks before a show. The boss's internal alarm clock goes off, and all of a sudden the trade show, left to the last minute, escalates in importance. Many things can, and usually do, go awry: the graphics are wrong; the booth is worn out; new products and catalogs aren't ready; hotels are booked; Supersaver airfares are sold out. Sound familiar?

Scenarios such as these exemplify why it's crucial to develop a timetable for your preshow planning. Planning should begin as early as possible. Some companies plan 18 to 24 months in advance. Although you may not always have that luxury, I do recommend 12 months. A game-plan countdown follows.

T Minus Twelve Months

- Evaluate available shows for selection.
- Choose space and send in contract with deposit.
- Analyze the show. Who will attend? What is the general theme?
- Begin planning show. Assemble your show team for a planning session. Develop your objectives. Put them on paper.
- Establish a show budget.

T Minus Eleven Months

- Make hotel reservations. Be sure to allow for inevitable personnel changes. Hotels don't like that, but then, they overbook, too, don't they?
- Make airline reservations.
- Assign booth personnel. Remember, this is not a training ground for rookies, nor is it a vacation.

T Minus Ten Months

- Begin planning display. Can your old one be refurbished, or do you need a new one?
- Consult with display builders.
- Check show regulations to make sure your plans are within procedures.

T Minus Nine Months

- Finalize booth design. Does it need show management approval? Don't just arbitrarily build an exhibit and assume you can use it. Make sure you have permission to put it up.
- Have another planning session with your show team.

T Minus Eight Months

- Review your budget. Make sure it is still realistic.
- Consult with display builder. Make sure the company is on schedule.

T Minus Seven Months

- Work with show team on products for display. Does this need to be coordinated with your production or design departments?
- Bring in members of the advertising department. Update them on the project and get them started planning publicity and promotion tied into general show theme.

T Minus Six Months

- Consult with display builder on status. Finalize any design and graphics not already done.
- Check on any company literature to be used for show. Is it appropriate for this particular show? Do you have sufficient quantity?
- Order any supplies and equipment needed for the show.
- Contact restaurants in trade show vicinity for reservations for each night during show. Make enough for show staff and guests.

T Minus Five Months

- Review exhibitor kit (if it has arrived) sent from the show management. Fill out any forms requesting product information, program listing, or promotional materials.
- Fill out advanced registration forms for all your personnel.
- Meet with show team for updates and status reports.

T Minus Four Months

- Work with advertising department to issue press releases, new product introductions, and promotional materials to news media.

- Meet with van line representative to arrange for shipment of all exhibit materials, sample products, display, and literature.
- Arrange for training for floor selling.

T Minus Three Months

- Submit all necessary forms for services (furniture, carpets, cleaning, electricity, labor, telephone, computer, security, etc.). Prepay if possible to get preshow discounts.
- Begin preshow marketing campaign to stimulate attendance.
- Meet with show team for updates and status reports.

T Minus Two Months

- Reconfirm hotel and airline reservations.
- Finalize booth personnel, schedules, and assignments.
- Put together your company's personalized exhibit staff manual (covered in Chapter 3).
- Meet with show team for updates and status reports.
- Accelerate your preshow marketing program. (See Chapter 4.) Mail personalized invitations to prospects and customers.

T Minus One Month

- Put up your display for inspection and last-minute adjustments.
- Double-check to make sure show service forms were sent.
- Insure your exhibit.
- Work with your transportation people for a final check on all arrangements.
- Ship exhibit materials, display, and literature to arrive on the first day space is available for receiving shipments.
- Preshow training programs for show staff should be confirmed.
- Put together all necessary office and sales supplies.
- Get traveler's checks for any on-site payments.

Launch

- Install exhibit on the first day your space is available. Be prepared to handle any last-minute problems.

- Confirm all show orders for labor and rentals.
- Conduct preshow training and rehearsals.
- Take care of any last-minute crises.

Mission Control

- Conduct daily meetings to evaluate show progress and assess any changes needed.
- Keep the booth clean.
- Arrange for exhibit teardown after show.
- Arrange for next year's space, if possible.

Mission Debriefing

- Oversee teardown and packing.
- Evaluate results of leads generated at show and distribute leads as soon as possible.
- Evaluate overall company performance.
- Begin new planning countdown for next year's show.

It takes some time to fill out all necessary information and project deadlines, but you'll be glad you did. As the show approaches, you won't have all those last-minute rush orders to sweat over. By having this countdown posted on your wall or in a trade show workbook, you'll be able to refer to it easily, maintain a schedule, and demonstrate your professionalism.

CHAPTER 3

Coordinating the Show

The Exhibit Planning Handbook

Having mastered the trade show time line, we turn now to another valuable aid to your show success, the Exhibit Planning Handbook. You will need a three-ring binder (preferably at least two inches wide) divided into eight sections. This notebook will keep all your planning organized and logical. Each of the eight sections is described in detail below.

Planning

This section includes your time line, budget, notes or minutes of show team meetings, show objectives, and any other material pertinent to the planning process.

Exhibit

This section contains any information about the exhibit and its graphics, including setup instructions, pictures or line drawings of what the final setup should look like, provisions for quick repairs, and emergency numbers.

Show Services

This section holds copies of all show orders—labor, electricity, rentals, telephone, cleaning, and the like. Also keep photocopies of any checks written for these services.

Promotion

This section includes copies of ads, direct mail pieces, mailing lists, ad schedules, and anything used in the marketing and advertising campaign for the show.

Shipping

This section includes copies of bills of lading, the PRO number or air bill number, the trailer number or flight number, the name of the delivering carrier (if different from your original carrier), the telephone number of your carrier representative in your hometown, the telephone number of the carrier representative at the show site, transfer points and phone numbers, and the telephone number of the terminal show destination.

On Duty

This section includes all information related to your show staff, show training, and the like. Include a complete copy of the *Exhibit Staff Manual,* outlined later in this chapter.

Lead Fulfillment

This section contains copies of lead generation forms and any plans and objectives on lead conversion.

Miscellaneous

This section holds anything related to the trade show that isn't included in the previously described categories. By compiling this information and putting it in your own Exhibit Planning Handbook, you will be accomplishing three important objectives:

1. You will have everything conveniently located in one place. You can take it with you to the show or give it to whomever is in charge at the

show. Not only does this make your job easier, but it makes you look more professional, too.
2. Any postshow report you make to your boss can include this manual. Your boss will be impressed.
3. The manual is a historical document that can serve as a guideline for future shows.

At this point, it is important to consider the issues of staff coordination and the use of an *Exhibit Staff Manual*.

The Exhibit Staff Manual

Show planning involves a number of people—corporate management, exhibit manager, sales manager, and sales staff. But don't forget your other support staff, the people back in the office. You need to include them in the planning as well as the implementation. During the show's planning stages, especially during meetings, include those who might have some valuable input and those who will be affected by the show. This includes secretaries, assistants, production and design staff, marketing and advertising personnel, and also upper management who might not be attending the show. Be sure everybody understands the importance of the show, as well as the show objectives. Doing so will ensure more complete cooperation and smoother teamwork. This, in turn, makes for better communication within your company—and better service outside.

Every staffer going to the show should get an *Exhibit Staff Manual*. Much like a playbook for a professional football team, the staff manual includes the who, what, when, where, and why of the show. Following are some of the areas you'll want to cover:

- Who will be working the booth
- Where they will be staying
- A map showing the convention hall and vicinity
- Names, addresses, and phone numbers of show facilities
- How messages will be handled
- Explanations of preshow advertising and promotions
- A map of the hall layout with your exhibit location
- A diagram of your exhibit layout
- A list of products to be displayed
- Staff work schedule

- Who will be attending conferences, and when
- New product information
- Product pricing structure
- Corporate objectives for the show
- Individual job assignments
- Personal objectives for staff members to fill out
- How to qualify prospects
- How to handle sales leads
- Printed collateral material to be distributed
- Information about daily staff meetings
- Information about entertaining customers/prospects
- Dealing with the press
- Teardown and departure procedures
- Return shipping

Your handbook should be highly confidential. Make sure that everybody receiving one understands the importance of knowing where it is at all times. Stress the importance of protecting the manual from prying eyes.

Creating the Ultimate Exhibit

So your last exhibit had a rotating stage for the magician, laser beams streaking overhead, and models distributing handouts? Gee, I don't understand why you didn't get any sales, either. Be serious, folks. Such antics are useless. Good booth design focuses on the product and increases legitimate show traffic *without* ridiculous gimmicks. If there is a main purpose for your booth, it's to attract the specific prospects you seek. This goal should be foremost in your mind when designing an exhibit.

I highly recommend using a professional service to help you design and build your exhibit; nonetheless, you will want to be as prepared for them as possible. By understanding the various aspects of booth design and how they relate to your own needs, you will be in a better position to communicate with the designer.

Booth Dimensions

This factor depends on your show budget, desired objectives, available show space, and personnel capabilities. Budget is the biggest factor. Unfortunately, most of us don't have the luxury of an unlimited budget, and exhibits range in cost from as low as $1,000 (for a small tabletop with no graphics) to as high as $1 million (for an elaborate, custom megabooth). Your budget will probably fall somewhere in between.

Like most of us, you probably don't control your budget and will have to settle for a 10-foot display. That's OK; just keep in mind that the size of your exhibit has a direct bearing on the results of your show. For example, if your major objective at a show is to generate new leads, the amount of actual leads you can generate will be affected by this limited space.

An exhibit generally occupies approximately 30 percent of your available space. In a 10-foot by 10-foot booth (100 square feet), your exhibit will cover approximately 30 square feet. That leaves only 70 square feet for exhibitors and attendees. The average person will use approximately 25 square feet of personal space. (This number derives from our penchant, as human beings, to "own" a certain amount of space around us, usually extending as far as the length of our arms; thus the phrase, "arm's-length transaction.")

Going back to our high school math, we remember that the area of a circle is represented by the formula:

Area = pi × (radius of circle) squared

In this example, pi is equal to 3.14, and the radius is equal to 3. By inserting these values, we now have:

Area = 3.14 × (3) squared = 3.14 × 9 = 28.26 sq. ft.

If you have 70 square feet of space available for people, at 25 square feet per person, then approximately three people fit in your booth, including salespeople. With two salespeople in this booth, allowing space for one attendee, it would still be crowded.

Now, by assuming your salespeople average six contacts per hour for a 30-hour show, your total potential contacts for the show number 360:

2 salespeople × 6 contacts/hour × 30 hours = 360 total show contacts

This figure is totally independent of the size of the show. It doesn't matter whether the show attracts 100,000 people or 1,000 people. With a 10-foot booth, you can only contact 360 attendees.

If you're fortunate enough to have a large budget, you can work backward from your objectives to determine the size of your exhibit. If you want 3,000 contacts, divide that number by the total show hours. We'll use 30 again; that's 100 contacts per hour. If salespeople make six contacts per hour, you need 17 salespeople (100 divided by 6). Seventeen salespeople each occupy 25 square feet, for a total of 425 square feet. Of course, if each of them is working with an attendee, you need to double the required space to 850 square feet, which equals 70 percent of the exhibit space. The other 30 percent contains the exhibit itself. Extrapolating these numbers, you find you need a booth of approximately 1,200 square feet to accommodate your objectives, a booth approximately 40 feet by 34 feet—that's a big booth.

Booth Location

This debate continues to rage on. Many so-called "experienced" show people will tell you that the best location in a show is near the front and center of the exhibition hall. The fact is, there has never been a study whose conclusion supports that. To address that issue, CEIR published a report (#SM/RR20), "The Effect of Booth Location on Exhibit Performance and Impact." It found that being located front and center wasn't advantageous in terms of booth traffic. And in a July 15, 1998, poll of *Tradeshow Week* magazine readers, nearly four in 10 respondents said that preshow promotion generates the most traffic, regardless of where the booth is located.

Secondly, for several years now, I have spoken before thousands of trade show attendees and have facilitated hundreds of focus groups for expositions. At every one of these opportunities, I have asked these straightforward questions: How much of the show floor do you walk, and how much does exhibit location affect your decision to visit a particular exhibitor? With only a handful of exceptions, the overwhelming response has been, "I walk the *entire* show, and location has *little* effect on my decision to stop."

Thirdly, to support a recurring theme in this book, do you want *everybody* in your booth or the *right* people? There are too many other, more important factors influencing an attendee's decision to stop in your exhibit. Did you aggressively use preshow promotion to let your target market know that you would be at the show? Is your exhibit designed to attract only those people you want to spend time with, or does it attract everybody? And, on top of all that, you are strictly limited to the size of your exhibit and the number of carefully trained staffers, as to the potential number of people you can talk to, anyway. Trying to get as many people in your booth as possible is a silly exercise in busyness, not effectiveness.

Here are some factors for you to consider:

- Don't be afraid of your competitors; you're all in the same place, any-way. Good buyers will examine all of you, and if you ever have the opportunity to clearly establish an advantage over your competitors, this is it! It provides an opportunity to toot your own horn.
- If you use gas or water, get near the source.
- Get to know the show management. They'll have a good feel for traf-fic flow and can help you select a location.
- Avoid dead ends; people just don't like them.
- Avoid food concession areas. The lines tend to back up, and you cer-tainly don't want them blocking your booth. Also, unless you've got a generic product, you're only trying to attract your specific target market, not every Tom, Dick, and Sherry.
- Watch for posts and columns located smack in the middle of your booth. Ask the show management for a floor plan.
- Watch for level changes. You won't want to work on a ramp during the whole show.

The Right Display

How do you plan to use the booth? Will it be used just once for a special occasion, such as the introduction of a new product or the celebration of a corporate anniversary? A custom design might suit such purposes. Or do you plan to use it 15 times a year for the next five years? If so, you need to build something durable, easy to transport, and easy to assemble.

What other uses do you have for your display? Will it be stored between shows, or will it be used in your office lobby? Maybe you'll take it to shopping mall shows as well as industry trade shows. The more you can define the uses for your exhibit in advance, the fewer headaches you'll experience later.

Several different types of exhibits are available for consideration:

- *Tabletop.* These exhibits are designed for display atop a six- or eight-foot table. They're easy to set up, take down, and transport. They are also the least expensive.
- *Portable display.* Like the tabletop exhibit, these are easy to set up, take down, and transport; their advantage is they stand alone. A portable is easily carried, and its size allows it to be checked as luggage on an airplane.

- *Modular display*. The structural elements are interchangeable, providing maximum flexibility in arrangement and size. A 20-foot display, for example, can be broken down into two 10-foot displays.
- *Custom display*. Specifically designed and built for the user, it is usually the most expensive of all displays built.
- *Rental display*. A complete package offered through a trade show on a rental basis.
- *Used display*. A previously owned and used display.

The type of exhibit you use depends largely on your needs and budget. Be forewarned; it's easy to buy more than you need. Determine your objectives and budget before you sit down with an exhibit house or independent designer, then stick to your plan.

The Name of the Game

The sole purpose of your exhibit is to attract the attention of your target market attendees. However, many companies get caught in the identity trap at trade shows. Their booths display huge signs that trumpet the company name and corporate logo. Unless your name is already highly recognizable—IBM, Sony, General Motors—no one will be affected by it. Your message should be simple, effective, and list an important benefit to your target market. The structure should not compete with the message, nor should it overpower the all-important products on display.

When creating a new booth, keep the following design components in mind:

- *Color*. Neutral colors work best in the display mix. Brighter colors tend to show wear and tear more easily.
- *Graphics*. Use a minimal amount of graphics and make them large and easy to read.
- *Lighting*. Good overall lighting is a must. Attention is drawn to well-lit objects; highlight your message and product effectively with the exhibit lighting.
- *Display counters*. Exhibits that are countertop level are easier on the attendees' eyes and alleviate the need to bend over the booth. Demonstrations are also more easily performed at chest height.
- *Maintenance*. A clean and attractive booth is much more conducive to business. Be sure that the booth is easy to maintain and kept clutter-free.

- *Photos.* A single large photo is much more attractive and effective than a series of smaller pictures.
- *Audiovisuals.* Can audiovisuals be incorporated into the design for maximum impact and memorability?
- *Demonstrations.* Does your display allow enough space for effective demonstrations? Is it designed to enhance the demonstration?
- *Transportability.* Is the booth easily transportable? Can you carry it yourself, or do you need to have it shipped?
- *Carpet.* Do you need your own carpeting, or can you rent it as needed to match your exhibit?

Generating Leads—and Capturing Customers

Several years ago, as national sales manager for a Japanese toy company, I made sure we participated in as many regional and national trade shows as possible. I was convinced that trade shows were a great place to get new leads. We traveled around the country, exhibiting and talking to thousands of enthusiastic prospects. And, like most companies, we sent off business cards to our independent reps with visions of millions of dollars in orders rolling in. To our surprise (and chagrin), the avalanche of new customers never materialized. In fact, over several months, they barely represented a trickle. Having invested a tremendous amount of time and money to go to these shows, we were understandably disappointed and confused. What happened to all those enthusiastic prospects? Where were the orders we expected?

We knew an analysis of the situation was necessary. Like any good sales manager, I blamed the sales reps. After all, I slaved at all those shows, collecting business cards, sleeping in airports, living out of my suitcase, just so I could send them thousands of leads. Something had to be wrong with them. So I called the reps and asked what happened to all those great leads? Where were the sales? The responses from the reps surprised me:

"I drove all over my territory to see the first six people on the list. They had no intention of buying anything. Because it was a total waste of my time, I tossed the rest of the leads in one of my desk drawers."

"I learned a long time ago that trade show leads aren't worth anything. I never bother to follow up. I've got better things to do with my time."

"The list of leads you gave me contained no information about those prospects. How was I to know what you showed them or discussed at the show? It would be just like making cold calls."

"By the time you sent the leads to me, these people had already made their decisions. You waited too long."

At first I was upset with the reps, feeling they were just plain lazy. I blamed them for the failure of the trade show program. Fortunately, I realized there was something to their statements. Maybe I was missing something.

I began a more in-depth study of trade show sales leads. I asked the reps to tell me what information they wanted about leads. What could a show staff do to make leads more valuable? What would turn those leads into sales?

From talking with the reps, I learned that we needed to pay more attention to providing them with qualified inquiries. I realized there were actually two ways to qualify a show inquiry. The first was to continue working shows the way we had, and then hire a telemarketing firm to call all the leads generated to prioritize them in order of buying time frame. Then we would send only qualified leads to reps. The second, and most expedient, way to qualify inquiries was to have the floor staff do it right at the show. We felt this was the best way to go, but more information was still needed.

I spoke with current customers, asking them what they looked for at trade shows. How could an exhibitor know whether they were going to buy or not? I talked to our reps, asking them what information they needed to help close the sale. I talked with show managers, asking for more information about the attendees at various shows. I called the Trade Show Bureau and asked for information about how to make shows more effective. I even talked to other exhibitors (including competitors), asking them how they handled new leads.

This informal but enlightening survey led me to a number of insights and conclusions:

1. Everybody in the loop must buy into your program for it to be a success. Qualified lead generation and fulfillment require the

cooperation of the exhibit and field staff, the sales reps (whether in-house or independent), and the buyers.

2. A business card is not a qualified lead. Although it does not take a mental giant to figure this out, many companies still use this method to collect leads. I used to be guilty of it. Lead forms need to be designed to include enough room for proper data collection. And don't plan on writing information on the back of business cards. They just aren't big enough.

3. The exhibit and field staff require proper training to approach, qualify, and rate prospects during a very short time frame at the show—so short, in fact, I now call it "The 9½ Minute Sales Call."

4. The sales reps need to be prepared to follow up and report on qualified trade show leads. Lead follow-up begins in the home office, using direct mail and telemarketing. Leads should be followed up in a timely manner and then dispensed to the proper rep.

5. Once a lead has been assigned to a rep, a tracking system must be implemented to encourage and demand timely follow-up.

6. A word-processing and database management system is a must for immediate follow-up, field assignments, and future communications.

Once I came to these conclusions, we were able to implement a more effective trade show lead conversion program. The first thing we did was outline a show lead form. From my research we were able to determine what information was needed on the form:

1. Complete identification of the prospect, including name, company, address, phone, fax number (if available), and company profile.

2. Specific product interest and area or use.

3. Budget and buying time frame.

4. Other possible buying influences. Who else might be involved in the decision-making process?

5. Comments from prospect—specific objections, concerns, special situations, requests, and so on.

6. Name of trade show and dates held.

7. Information for postshow follow-up. Do they need a personal call? Did they request literature? Do they need a sample?

8. Personal comment about prospect. Did he wear a great-looking tie at the show? Did she mention her recent vacation to Europe? This information is used in follow-up letters to add a personal touch.

9. Name and signature of person filling out lead form.

10. A rating system for handling and prioritizing inquiries. We came up with a simple 1, 2, 3 system for rating leads. A 1-rated lead was

super-hot and required immediate follow-up. A 2-rated prospect was considered warm. We sent requested literature with a cover letter, but followed up with a phone call to requalify before making a personal sales call. All 3-rated contacts were put on our in-house mailing list; if they showed more interest, we elevated them to 2-status. We only sent 1- and 2-rated leads to our reps. Using this rating system also helped us set objectives for each show. For example, we might go to one show with a goal of reaching 20 new 1-rated leads and 150 new 2-rated leads.

11. Follow-up report information for tracking.

Once we came up with the ingredients for the show form, we put them together and came up with a long version of the lead tracking form shown in Figure 3-1. Customize this form to fit your company's needs. The important thing is to use the form completely. The few minutes it takes to fill it out will not only answer many questions, but, in the long run, it will save you and your staff valuable time.

I designed the lead form to fit on an easy-to-handle sheet of paper, about 3½ inches wide by 8½ inches long. That way your staffers can easily carry it. I also had it photocopied on card stock for easier use.

The form was designed for easy tracking. All follow-ups are written and dated. Before a lead is sent to a field rep, we photocopy it for our tickler files. That way we can track each lead individually and check on progress. The nuts and bolts of postshow follow-up will be discussed in more detail in Chapter 8.

An old but classic story concerns an exhibitor who went to a trade show with the objective of collecting leads. Every day at the end of the show he carefully secured the day's leads in a locked cabinet. At the following year's show, the same cabinet was set up at the back of the booth and unlocked. You guessed it, the leads from the previous year were still secure. As I stated, it's an old story, but certainly one to keep in mind. Remember—it doesn't matter how many leads you get, if you don't do anything with them. Design a lead tracking form, then use it!

Preparing the Staff

Of course, all this planning doesn't benefit anyone if the people involved don't know what's going on. Both the exhibit staff and field reps need to be trained and educated on how to maximize their effectiveness before, during, and after the trade show. It's just as important for them to understand the *why* as it is for them to understand the *what*. If you want your exhibit and field staff to support your show efforts enthusiastically, you'll want to do the same.

Most people think of trade show training as just boothmanship—the basic do's and don'ts of working an exhibit. It's more than that. Boothmanship only covers the actual floor selling process, not preshow or postshow efforts. I've already established the importance of developing the correct perception of exhibiting, preshow and postshow planning, and marketing; it stands to reason that training and education should address these same areas.

Remember when I asked who taught you how to work a show? The same question can be put to your exhibit staffers. And the response would be the same. Odds are nobody has ever educated your salespeople and other exhibit workers on how to successfully staff an exhibit. They learned by watching other, equally uneducated staffers.

This is a major problem for you. The fact is your staffers are the most important factor in your exhibiting success. Nothing else you do will have as much of a positive or negative impact on your show results as your staff.

Besides lack of training, there are three other reasons why exhibit staffers fail to work shows effectively. The first is that they typically have no clear objective of what they're supposed to accomplish during their shifts. Without specific and measurable objectives, they have no direction. Usually, communication from the home office is limited to an itinerary, show work schedule, and nod of encouragement.

Staffers need clear objectives, based on their own contributions to the overall show objectives. If you're looking for leads and have set an objective of 400 leads during a show, then break it down per staffer. That way, when someone knows he or she has a show quota of 48 prospects, they'll be more focused on getting the job done.

Staffers also fail because they are forced out of their comfort zone. Salespeople are used to working in the field (usually alone), and office workers rarely experience the frenetic pace and environment of a trade show. In both cases, they're surrounded by hundreds, possibly thousands of total strangers. They've got competitors across the aisle. The boss is looking over their shoulder, and their peers are scrutinizing every move. Well, that's what they *think*. Regardless of whether any of this is true or not, they are way out of their comfort zone. Without proper direction, they're lost.

Figure 3-1 Show Lead Form

(Front of form)

Trade Show _____

Rep Name _____

Date _____

1   2   3

Contact Name _____

Company Name _____

Address _____

City, State _____ Zip _____

Telephone _____

Fax _____

Company Profile _____

_____

_____

Product Interest

   A _____

   B _____

   C _____

   D _____

Area of Use _____

_____

Budget _____

Buying Time Frame _____

_____

Other Buying Influences

   Name _____

   Title _____

   Name _____

   Title _____

(Back of form)

Requests Personal Call _____ Date _____

Requests Literature _____

Requests Samples _____ Date_____

   Which Ones _____

Comments from Prospect _____

_____

_____

_____

Personal Comment about Prospect _____

_____

_____

_____

Recorded by _____

_____ Mailed Literature on _____

_____ Date _____

_____ Follow-Up Telephone Call on _____

_____ Date _____

Turned Over to Salesperson _____

Follow-up Reports

Date _____

_____

Date _____

_____

Date _____

_____

Date _____

_____

Date _____

_____

The third reason why staffers fail is from preconceived notions. Unfortunately, it's common for "experienced" staffers to develop negative attitudes about the value of trade shows. "Well, we've got to be there, but it's a big waste of my time." When these experienced staffers get a hold of a new worker, I call those people "dogs with fleas." When a dog with fleas comes in contact with a dog without fleas, soon you've got two dogs with fleas. And, without a doubt, a preconceived negative attitude about trade shows can seriously impact your ultimate results.

The last reason why staffers fail is they confuse busyness with effectiveness. "Hey, I passed out 2,000 brochures. It must have been a successful show!" Yet, this type of activity is prevalent at every show.

Preshow Preparation

Make sure everyone understands what the company expects to gain from the trade show and what their individual responsibilities are. Then elaborate on how to accomplish show objectives. Everybody involved in the trade show must understand these objectives. During the period of 2 to 12 months before the show, send everybody a monthly status report. From 2 months on in, send reports weekly. They can be short, even one page; the point is to make team members feel they are an important part of the planning process. They then become an integral part of the show's success.

Another preshow sales tactic is to call targeted prospects for preshow contact; sales reps can often provide a list of past and potential buyers. Hold weekly pep rallies to encourage staff to get on the phone and make show appointments. Prizes and incentives awarded for confirmed appointments are important motivational tools. If your staff needs training in telephone skills, there are a number of excellent telemarketing programs available. If you have a large budget, hire an outside consultant to put on a customized training session. If you happen to know of one in your area, great. If not, I highly recommend George Walther, author of the top-selling books *Phone Power, Power Talking,* and *Upside-Down Selling.* George is one of the premier telemarketing consultants in the world and, in my opinion, one of the best speakers and trainers. If you don't have the budget to bring George in personally, he has a complete line of audio and video albums. Here's how to contact him:

George Walther
Speaking From Experience, Inc.
6947 Coal Creek, #100
Newcastle, WA 98059
425/255-2900
Fax 425/235-6360
E-mail GeoWalther@aol.com

(Be sure to say I told you to call. I don't get any commission from this recommendation, but maybe he'll give you a good deal.)

On-Site Preparation

Most companies make the mistake of assuming there is little difference between normal field sales and trade show sales. As a result, they don't see a need for any special training for themselves or their booth staff. Unfortunately for them, there is a vast difference between field sales and trade show sales.

In field sales, you go to the client; in trade show sales, the client comes to you. Typically, when a sales rep makes a call on a client or prospect, the rep must go to the client's office. Not only is this time-consuming, but there is a certain loss of control of the situation; this doesn't happen at a trade show. Where else will potential buyers just wander into your arms?

In the field, you're on their turf. In a trade show, they are on yours. When you call on a prospect, a certain amount of intimidation arises from being on someone else's turf. You aren't familiar with the surroundings. They can make you wait in the lobby, see drop-in visitors, and take phone calls. It can be uncomfortable. At a trade show, you control the environment—your booth. Yes, there are distractions; a trade show can be noisy. But you can set up your booth any way you want. You can design it to look like your office, the great outdoors, or even your production line. Because you control the environment, to a certain extent you control the prospects.

In the field, it's just you and the buyer. At a trade show, it's you and everybody else. Trade shows are like shopping malls. Prospects can come into your booth and listen to your sales pitch, then walk to your competition's booth to compare products. They discover almost immediately whether your products stack up against the competition. Are you as good, better, worse, cheaper, more expensive, longer lasting, more reliable, or guaranteed? When you're in their office, it's easier to claim your product is superior. At a trade show, you've got to be able to stand behind your claims because they can be tested immediately. It's imperative that you know exactly what you're talking about.

In the field, it's not always possible to demonstrate your product. If you sell heavy equipment, such as telephone interconnect systems, mainframe computers, or aircraft engines, it's just not possible to bring your product to the customer for an on-site demonstration. Conversely, a trade show is perfect for demonstrations. You can give a hands-on demonstration of your new time-management software; you can put cross sections of products on display for easy inspection; even custom demonstrations can be arranged to show your products in their best light.

In the field, you can't be in two places at once. At a trade show, it's possible for you to demonstrate and sell your product to more than one prospect at a time. Studies have shown that, on average, you will see more customers and prospects in three days at a show than you'll see in six months in the field.[1]

Trade show selling takes us out of our comfort zones. Any type of selling is uncomfortable, but measured in degrees, trade show selling is among the most difficult. It's only natural for people to spend time with people they like and know. Sales reps are no different— they spend more time and make more sales calls on old clients, customers, and even prospects. It's hard to get salespeople to make cold calls or to follow up on leads they are given. For the same reason, it's uncomfortable to work trade shows. The booth staff sees more new faces in three or four days of a trade show than they see all year in the field.

Through boothmanship training, members of the sales staff learn the differences between field sales and trade show sales; they learn how to utilize such differences to their advantage. They learn how to approach prospects and qualify them quickly. They learn how to efficiently, effectively, and professionally work a trade show to help your business reach its objectives.

---

[1] According to William Mee, President-Emeritus of the Trade Show Bureau.

Alternatives to Exhibiting

If your company supports all your extensive, expensive plans, your budget is approved, and you have enough people to staff the booth efficiently and effectively, congratulations! Unfortunately, for many of us, that's a pipe dream. You may not be in a position to spend big money at a trade show just yet. Maybe you only want to check out the show for possible future participation. Maybe the show is so popular that you can't get a space. Maybe you don't feel the show warrants spending a lot of money on a booth. Yet, even if you were only to rent a 10-foot space and run the show yourself, expenses could reach several thousand dollars.

Working a trade show doesn't have to be a black-and-white issue of whether you exhibit or not. Just because you've decided not to exhibit at a particular show doesn't mean you can't take advantage of it. After all, many of your major buyers will all be in one location for several days. Work the show anyway, even if you don't rent space. Although many companies claim to do this, they really aren't any different from the company that puts up a booth and waits for customers to flock because they don't plan ahead. They don't set show objectives or make appointments with customers and prospects. They just go to the show and walk around, and in so doing, they miss the many ways to take advantage of a show.

The Trade Show as Sales Call

When you call on a current customer or new prospect, you have to make an appointment. If you know that several of your clients or prospects will be attending a particular trade show, call them. Explain that your company won't be exhibiting at the show, but you plan to be in town to attend. Suggest getting together for a short meeting. Unless you call the day before the show and the prospect's time is all booked, they will say yes. After all, they are attending the show to meet with people like you. Just because you don't have a booth doesn't mean you can't meet with clients and prospects. Let's look at the benefits of this strategy.

Daily flexibility.   If you don't have an exhibit, you're not tied to a particular space. Because you don't have to be at an exhibit when the show opens, you can have a leisurely breakfast with a client. You can eat lunch anytime (many show staffers can't even take lunch) and leave the show anytime. Many attendees want to avoid the mad rush to the buses and taxis, so they'll leave early. Join them.

Moveability.   You can literally be a portable exhibit. Some shows are so big that buyers have to set up appointments in geographical clusters. A buyer may want to see you, but the only time available is Thursday morning at 10:15, when he's in the South Arena. No problem, because you aren't tied down.

Time management.   You needn't be out of touch with your office. Often it's difficult for show staff to contact the home office and take care of other business. You don't have that problem because you organize your own day. Not only can you contact the office and reach customers by phone when you have to, but you can do it away from the noise of the show. Show-related appointments and other daily business duties don't have to clash.

Entertainment and hospitality.   If you require a place to meet with prospects, spend a few hundred dollars on a suite. If your suite is convenient to the show site, people will come when invited. You can even set up a display in the room if you have to. (Hospitality suites are discussed in more detail in Chapter 7.)

Less stress.   You won't have to set up a booth or tear it down, which also saves you from working with unions. You don't have to stay in a booth all day culling through strangers to find qualified buyers, so there's no need to stand for many hours and worry about proper body language.

Less cost.   An obvious reason, but an important factor is cost. You avoid the cost of the booth space, exhibit and graphics, freight, services, and advertising. You also save money on travel expenses because you can fly in as late as the day before the show begins and leave even before the show is over.

Check out the trends and competition.   When you're not on appointments, be sure to spend time walking the show. Visit your competition and see what's new. Also see who's visiting their booths; you might pick up some new leads. Be sure to cover the whole show.

Many of the newest products are brought out by small companies relegated to small 10-foot exhibits on the outside aisles or downstairs. Keep your eyes and ears open.

Work the show floor.   When walking through a show, I'm as conscious of the badges of people walking by me as I am of the booths. Many times I've run into prospects who, for one reason or another, weren't able to come by my booth. Because you don't have an exhibit, it's doubly important for you to be aware of people around you. Look for possible contacts on the bus, in the cafeteria, in your competition's booth, at the shoe shine stand, even in the rest rooms. Keep your eyes and ears open.

Seminars and workshops.   Without an exhibit, you have the flexibility of adjusting your schedule to attend speeches and programs. This is important to your continuing education in your field. Furthermore, these sessions are heavily attended by buyers.

A bonus reason.   Something magical happens on the last day of the show: Usually a short day, it becomes a big, indoor swap meet. I've seen people pushing shopping carts up and down aisles to buy samples at rock-bottom prices. Who needs it? And because you don't have an exhibit, you don't have to stay!

Don't misinterpret me. I'm not saying that these practices are superior to having a booth at the show. But, if after careful analysis, you decide not to exhibit, then consider working the show this way. In many ways, it's just as exhausting as having a booth, but for less cost, it might also be just as rewarding.

CHAPTER 4

Preshow Marketing

The Trade Show Rule

Typically, trade show management will predict more attendees than the hall can hold. On the afternoon of the first day, however, you can shoot a cannon down the aisles. And, keep in mind that most exhibitors in shows with 100,000-plus attendance assume that only 20,000 to 30,000 of the attendees are legitimate buyers—if they're lucky. In other words, only 25 percent of the people walking into your booth are real buyers of something. You *still* have to target those who fit your target market!

Consider this last example further. If the show is open for a total of 30 hours over four days, you might be able to average about 12 contacts per hour—360 total initial contacts. If 25 percent of them are legitimate buyers, that's only 90 real contacts. Then let's say that half of those actually fit your target market. If you were going to a show with 100,000 attendees and I said that you would come away with only 45 leads, would you think I was crazy? Yet that is a realistic example of what you might be able to accomplish at a show.

This brings us to what I call *The Trade Show Rule:*

> The ultimate success of your trade show lies entirely with you and has nothing, repeat, *nothing* to do with show management.

Of course, right now you're shaking your head and quietly saying to yourself, "This guy's crazy. The management of *our* trade show is very involved in bringing buyers in. Why, I just saw a large ad in our industry's trade magazine inviting buyers to the show."

That may be true. But before you close this book and donate it to Goodwill, let's discuss what you can expect from trade show management.

Trade show managers are running a business. Their product is the trade show and their measure of success is how many square feet of floor space they sell. The more floor space they sell, the more successful they are. And the way they ensure the continued success of the show is to make exhibitors happy. Somewhere along the line, someone decided that the total number of people attending a trade show determines its success, and for some strange reason, the exhibitors went along with this. After all, if 25,000 buyers attend a show and you don't get any sales, it must be *your* fault. So, the bigger the attendance, the happier the exhibitors. The happier the exhibitors, the more successful the show. The more successful the show, the faster the companies sign up for next year. Thus the mirage perpetuates itself.

The catch is that sheer attendance has *nothing* to do with success at a trade show. Your success is unique to your company and may be based on many factors: sales, new prospects, developing relationships with customers, product testing, and market research, to name a few. I seriously doubt that you define 25,000 attendees as an objective.

The preshow marketing help you can expect from show management includes promoting the event through direct mail, trade magazine ads, and ticket promotions (sometimes). These marketing efforts are aimed at a broad audience in order to attract large numbers of attendees. Somewhere within that large group of attendees may be your target market, but it is up to you to determine if this is so, and, if it is, to attract the right people to your booth. Remember, show management guarantees attendance, not buyers.

Ensuring Your Success
Before You Go

Preshow marketing can determine your success or failure at the show at the most fundamental level: If your target customers don't know you're going to be at the trade show, how can they be expected to look for your booth? Do you really believe that you can just rent booth space, put your exhibit up, and wait for the crowds? In a study for the Center for Exhibition Industry Research (formerly the Trade Show Bureau), six factors were identified as influencing a prospect's decision to visit a selected exhibit.[1]

[1]"Trade Show Bureau Research Report No. 13," July 1982.

1. Interesting product demonstrations: 28 percent. An attendee is attracted by top quality, professional demonstrations. This doesn't necessarily mean using professional models, actors, or actresses; it simply means demonstrations presented in an interesting, appealing fashion.
2. Exhibit location: 23 percent. Obviously, it's much better to be as close to the front and center of the exhibition hall as possible. Even though this appears to contradict what I wrote in Chapter 3 on booth location, it doesn't. The first reference is to booth traffic throughout the show. Location should not affect traffic. This study refers to the reason why an attendee visited a specific exhibit. Although buyers do, in fact, walk through an entire show, it is unlikely they visit a specific company against the back wall on a lower level because of the location. And think about this—if the only reason people stop in your booth is because of location, what does that say about their perception of your company and your salespeople?
3. Associate recommendation: 22 percent. One of the most powerful means of getting people to come to your booth is by having your customers and professional contacts arrange for prospects to visit.
4. Exhibit presentation: 13 percent. The three things an attendee sees first are the exhibit, the products, and the personnel. These three factors work together to form your exhibit's presentation. Make sure they're good.
5. Sales rep recommendation: 12 percent. Salespeople know the names and addresses of their target market and can extend personal invitations to its members. The prospects then know what you're displaying and where you're located.
6. Exhibit size: 2 percent. The sheer size of an exhibit is enough to create curiosity for a booth.

Other than the obvious reason of drawing people to your booth at a trade show, there is one more compelling reason for using preshow marketing. It helps stretch out the show. Typically, a company treats a trade show as a two- to five-day event, depending on its length, with the focus almost entirely on making those few days as productive as possible. This approach utilizes only one-third of a show's potential marketing power. A trade show is actually utilized at its fullest in a four- to five-month campaign, with the show situated in the middle. A trade show has three definite time frames—before, during, and after. Each of those has its own unique marketing forte. By effectively tying your marketing campaign in with the upcoming show two to three months before its opening, you can create enthusiasm and anticipation for the event, emphasizing exciting, new products and services you'll be offering. This not only stimulates your customers and prospects, but your employees as well. Then, by working an exciting show followed by a high-powered postshow campaign, the result will most certainly be a successful synergy. In short, a strong preshow marketing campaign ensures the success of a show before the show opens.

Several different methods can be utilized in a preshow campaign. How to implement some of these methods encompasses the remainder of this chapter.

Personal Prospecting

By far the most effective way to reach potential attendees is through personal invitations. Every survey and focus group I've supervised for trade show and corporations supports this. After giving a seminar to the exhibitors of the Food Marketing Institute's annual Supermarket Industry Convention, I led a panel discussion with several major buyers. They agreed that the best way to attract them to your booth was by sending personal letters (not something addressed "Dear FMI Attendee") along with a strong, motivating reason, specifically addressing their area of responsibility, suggesting why they would want to visit you.

The first step in this process is to identify your target audience and assemble a mailing list; include current customers and prospects. Assembling the current customer list is easy, but it will probably require extensive work to gather a prospect list. Several ways exist to gather these names and addresses. Your sales reps should know the names of several prospects they haven't been able to sell yet. You can also get mailing lists through reputable list brokers, a specific trade or professional association, a trade publication, even from the trade show itself. Be sure to ask only for the list segments most applicable to your target audience.

Once you've compiled these lists, start using them two to three months prior to the show. Begin with a personal invitation from the most prestigious person in the department (how about your company president?). Don't make the letter too long; just briefly tell them the name of the show, its dates, what products you'll be showing, why it would benefit them to visit you, where you will be located, and the name, address, and telephone number of someone to contact for more information. The important thing about personal invitations is just that: they are *personal*. The prospect feels cared for as an individual. Don't, therefore, send your invitations via bulk mail and don't stuff them full of product sheets and pricing information. Save that for the show.

One week after this initial letter, the contact person should follow up with personal phone calls, letters, and invitations to persuade prospects to visit your booth. Don't be satisfied with a mere confirmation that they'll visit the booth. Get even more personal and ask for an appointment. There are two good reasons for doing this. First is commitment; they have an obligation to show up since they set an appointment. Second, the salesperson responsible for that prospect can arrange to be in the booth for that appointment. Such appointments are key to trade show success. If every salesperson books an average of four appointments per hour, the show radiates success even before it opens. Primary goals are already accomplished; if anybody else comes into the booth, it's merely a perk.

Personal invitations don't work all the time. Sometimes you have to be a little more creative to get your prospect's attention, as shown in the following example.

A small Southern California toy company planned to exhibit at the New York Premium/Incentive Show. In researching the show, they discovered there were going to be more than 30,000 attendees. The sales manager was excited until he found out there would also be 1,500 other exhibitors. An added concern was the knowledge that Apple Computer would have a 1,200-square-foot exhibit across the aisle from them. The toy company feared its 100-square-foot booth would be dwarfed by the computer giant.

To get the attention of its prospects, the toy company put together a wave campaign to personally invite its target market and set up appointments. A wave campaign is a short-term series of coordinated marketing steps taken to accomplish a particular objective. In this case, the campaign was a three-stage mailing with each letter designed to generate interest in the next. Ten weeks prior to the show, the first letter—sent from the president—invited all prospects to visit them at the show. The second letter included a floor plan with the company's location clearly marked in red.

In the third mailing, knowing the attendees would be on their feet for four days, and that all that walking and standing would make for tired, sore feet, the sales manager sent a pair of

Dr. Scholl's footpads—with his corporate logo silkscreened right on the pad. If the prospects used the pad, every time they put their shoes on or took them off, they would see the toy company's logo. Follow-up phone calls two weeks before the show netted dozens of appointments. The number of drop-ins at the show was also high. The result of this creative and personal campaign? More than 90 percent of the targeted prospects visited the exhibit.

There is another method I've used several times when inviting specific people to my exhibits. I first utilized it after trying, with no success, to make a trade show appointment with the president of a Fortune 500 corporation. Although I didn't have a problem getting him on the phone, he maintained that his show schedule was already packed and he couldn't possibly see me; he just didn't have the time. I was waiting for a flight from Los Angeles to Chicago a couple of weeks prior to the show when an idea came to me. I went to the flight insurance counter and took out an insurance policy. I made the president of that company the beneficiary, attached a "thinking of you" note to it, and sent it to him. Two days later, after I returned from Chicago, he set the appointment. (Maybe he didn't want *me* to show up for the appointment.)

Telemarketing

So you don't have a big advertising budget. That's OK. It isn't necessary to spend a fortune to have an effective advertising campaign before a trade show because there are several types of advertising available. Remember, as you plan, think "collective advertising" and spread your ad dollars over more than one vehicle.

Telemarketing is the next best thing to personal invitations. If you currently use telemarketing in your marketing mix, then it will be easy to implement it in your preshow marketing plan. Simply compile a list of your targeted prospects and have your telemarketing staff phone for appointments six weeks prior to the show's opening.

If you do not use telemarketing in your business, you may be getting left behind. I strongly encourage you to research it through books, tapes, and seminars. A simple beginning, however, would be to compile your list of target prospects, then write a simple script. Here is an example:

Hello, may I speak with Mr./Mrs./Ms. _____?

Good morning/afternoon, Mr./Mrs./Ms. _____.

This is _____. I am calling for the Widget Manufacturing Company in Seattle. Are you planning to attend the National Premium Incentive Show in New York May 5 to 8?

(Pause)

(If no) We're sorry to hear that. We were looking forward to showing you _____. Will there be anyone else from your company whom we might be able to see?

(If no) Thanks anyway, Mr./Mrs./Ms. I'll make sure you still receive information about the _____. Goodbye.

(If yes to the first question) Great! We'd like very much to set up an appointment for you to visit our booth. Would Monday morning at 11:30 be all right, or would Tuesday afternoon at 2:00 be better for you?

(Pause)

(If they pick one) I've got you down to visit our exhibit on _____. I'll put a confirmation in the mail. Thank you for your time, Mr./Mrs./Ms. _____.

(If they don't want to set an appointment) I understand, Mr./Mrs./Ms. _____. Can we at least set up either Monday morning or Tuesday afternoon? (I've never been turned down for this.)

(Pause)

Fine, thank you so much. I'll pass on this information to Mr./Mrs./Ms. _____, who will be looking for you. Goodbye.

Such calls are simple and shouldn't take more than a few minutes. If you can't spare anyone to make those calls, hire temporary telemarketers. Give them the list and the script. You can pay them hourly or, better yet, pay them per appointment made.

Direct Mail

Next to personal invitations and telemarketing, direct mail is the best way to reach potential attendees. Compile a list of current clients, known prospects, people who have requested product information in the past 12 months, and other likely sources. Again, you can add to the number of names by purchasing a list from a reputable broker, business association, or trade publication.

Follow the same plan as that designed for personal invitations; but instead of personal follow-ups, send two or three mailings beginning three months before the show, spaced three to four weeks apart. Include a small premium or incentive to encourage them to visit your exhibit. There are literally thousands of ideas available, so don't just fall back on the standard pencil, calendar, or keychain. Get out your Yellow Pages and look up "Advertising Specialties" for a local distributor; then go visit the showroom and explain your objective and budget. The distributor should have plenty of samples and catalogs for you to choose from. This is a specialized industry; let the distributor help you.

If you do plan to use a premium or incentive, be sure to give the advertising specialty distributor plenty of time (at least four to six weeks) to get the products for you. Also, expect to put a 50 percent deposit down on your order. Unless the company has been working with you for some time, you probably can't avoid this.

Use your imagination when designing this series of mailings; obviously, the bigger your budget, the more options you have. A professionally produced audiotape inviting the prospect to visit you is a great idea. It's common practice for people to throw away junk mail before it's even read (especially if it's bulk mail), but I've never heard of anyone automatically throwing away an audiotape received in the mail.

Maybe you don't have a budget that will cover audiotapes, yet need something eye-catching. When you run your series of ads in the trade publication, ask the publisher to run off an extra thousand copies of the page with your ad. It's inexpensive, and you'll then be able to incorporate the ad in your direct mail campaign, including a note stating, "As seen in Widget Trade News."

Fax

Faxed invitations are a great way to contact your best prospects and customers. While fax machines probably have a short lifespan, it will still be a few years before they completely disappear.

Be careful, though—there is still a bit of a stigma in sending an unsolicited fax. Because sending a fax is fairly inexpensive, some companies go overboard. How many of us have had the fax machine taken up at 9:00 A.M. by an unwanted five-pager while we were waiting for something important? Some states are actually in the process of passing laws regarding unsolicited faxes.

None of this is meant to discourage you. If you're going to send faxes to potential trade show attendees, just keep a couple of simple rules in mind:

- Keep it short, no longer than one page. Besides not tying up their fax machine, your prospect has neither the time nor the inclination to read anything longer.
- Send it at night. Again, you're not tying up their machine during the day. In addition, your invitation will be the first thing on their desk in the morning. Faxes sent at the right time can really be attention-getters.

E-mail

FedEx wasn't fast enough. We had to have fax machines. But even that wasn't fast enough. Now we've got E-mail. Is this finally fast enough for us?

Promoting your participation at trade shows via E-mail can be tempting. The thought of instantly sending hundreds or thousands of personal invitations with the click of a button gives one a great sense of power and effectiveness. Sure, we can type up an invitation and send it quickly through the Internet, MCI Mail, CompuServe, America Online, Microsoft's forthcoming on-line system, or whatever gateway we have. Unfortunately, at the time of this writing, we're still a long way from being that well connected.

The advantage of E-mail is that it doesn't cost a lot of money or time. It's basically a local phone call. The bad news comes in two parts, though. The first is we're still communicating with people on a mass scale, not the rifle-shot approach that makes for an effective promotion. And the second is that we still don't have everybody's E-mail address. How do we contact those we most want to talk with?

However, this is certainly an area you need to pay close attention to. On-line services are here to stay. If you aren't part of this major revolution in communication technology, you will soon be left in the dust. Which brings me to the next area for potential preshow promotion.

Cyberspace

As Nicholas Negroponte, of MIT's Media Lab, puts it, the essence of the information revolution is the difference between atoms and bits. The former are the building blocks for physical stuff, which until now have formed the basis of our physical communications. Bits are evanescent; a big word for something so small. But from something so small, we have created the information age and a new way of communicating. Increasingly, our experiences are being shaped by the computer. More of our contact with customers, prospects, and suspects occurs through modems.

Will we be able to promote our own participation at trade shows through cyberspace? Maybe yes, maybe no. The singular problem of using the information highway is exactly the same as using trade shows to reach our target market. With thousands of potential exhibits to visit, how will our prospects find us? On-line services are the same thing. Unless someone already knows where we are and has a reason to connect with us on-line, we can't tell them to visit us at the trade show—sort of a cyber-Catch-22.

Of course, if you already have a well-attended website on the World Wide Web, by all means use that opportunity to invite your on-line visitors to meet you in person at the exposition. You can use that opportunity to create a page with photos of new products that will be displayed in your booth. You can scan in and upload a map of the show floor with your own location highlighted or blinking. Prospective customers can download an invitation to your hospitality suite. And they can even respond to an on-line survey about a new service you're planning on offering.

Literature

Trade publications are a good way to reach your target market; however, steer clear of show issues, especially if your ad budget is small. In the advertising world, it's better to employ frequency over size; that is, it's better to run a series of smaller ads for a few months before the show than to have a full-page, four-color ad in a show issue, even if the publisher passes out thousands of bonus copies at the show. A study conducted by Exhibit Surveys for the Center for Exhibition Industry Research shows booth traffic increases by about 40 percent for every four pages of preshow advertising.[2] It's my opinion that the show issue doesn't get read until after the show, if at all. Attendees at a show don't arrive, pick up show issues, and then sit down to read them before visiting booths. They set their schedule before walking into the arena. Be a part of their schedule by utilizing trade publications early and frequently.

Using Advertising Specialties as Show Promotions

Advertising specialties are the little handouts you see at every trade show, and there are literally thousands of possibilities. They represent one of the most powerful methods for creating brand awareness and name retention. At the same time, they are probably one of the most misunderstood and misused marketing tools available. The Advertising Specialty Institute was founded to help bring some semblance of order to a very confusing industry.

An item must meet three qualifications with regard to function, printed message, and price before it is defined as an advertising specialty.

Function

Those plastic bags given out by the millions at trade shows are a good example of an advertising specialty product. Their function is to hold things. They hold flyers, brochures, and other small giveaways. The problem with these bags is that they don't have a long life span. As soon as the stuff inside the bag is sorted, the bag is tossed out. These have become increasingly popular in recent years, which means there are probably several exhibitors at your show already doing this. Don't copy, innovate. I don't recommend plastic bags.

Imprinted with a Logo or Message

Every advertising specialty product will have a corporate logo or advertising message imprinted somewhere on its surface. Ways to imprint include silk screening, engraving, hot stamping, and printing.

[2]"Trade Show Bureau Research Report No. 27," October 1985.

Reasonable Cost

An advertising specialty product is usually fairly inexpensive, often just pennies per unit. If you plan to give every attendee walking by your booth a gift and there are 65,000 attendees, you don't want to spend very much. If, however, you're planning to give a nice gift to your top 100 customers at the show, you might want to spend a little more.

Customize Your Campaign!

Although I'm not necessarily endorsing the use of advertising specialty products, I do feel there is a place for them in a marketing mix. And, quite possibly, the trade show is a good place for them. If you elect to use giveaways, select something that will stand out in the crowd, something that will inspire your prospects to think well of you.

Personalize it.   Besides featuring your corporate logo, engrave the recipient's name on it. It adds a special, personal touch; also, people rarely throw out something imprinted with their name.

Ensure high perceived value.   One company used Swiss Army knives as part of an elaborate giveaway in a promotional campaign aimed at presidents of companies that purchased heavy equipment. Although compared to a truck costing hundreds of thousands of dollars the Swiss Army knife was inexpensive, the perceived value was high and the giveaway was a success because of the first-class campaign.

Build in exclusivity by limiting distribution.   My wife worked for Walker Manufacturing Company, a division of Tenneco. The company manufactures mufflers and catalytic converters. Like other automotive aftermarket companies, Walker uses several giveaway items—T-shirts, hats, knives, coffee cups, and jackets, to name a few, including a special black jacket that everybody wants. Not everybody gets one, however, because only a limited supply exists; it's become a special prize, a semi-status symbol among customers.

Cloak it in celebrity status.   After Jack Nicklaus won the Masters with an oversized putter, that particular brand reaped a sales bonanza. Everybody likes to have a product with such status behind it. If you can create status, capitalize on its value.

Provide a name-brand product or something designed by a renowned person.   Imagine giving away copies of a Leroy Neiman print specially painted for a customer's company. It would be even more successful if Neiman did the painting at the show.

Make it fit the taste, position, and status of the receiver.   Some companies keep using little gewgaws at trade shows to promote their name. The problem comes when they thrust one at a CEO in a $1,000 Giorgio Armani suit. Be careful and be sensitive to the receiver.

Flatter the receiver.   Create subtle awards that keep silently commending for years, and, of course, are seen by the right people. As an example: I have a paperweight in the shape of a star. I did a favor for a client and received it with my name engraved. It's proudly displayed on my desk for everybody to see. I've also seen companies use specially designed pens with the corporate logo imprinted as "medals of honor" for their salespeople. When somebody pulls out the special pen to write up an order, customers automatically know this salesperson is a winner.

Add a twist.   At one medical trade show, a company offered free teddy bears to every pediatrician invited to view a sales presentation. More than 93 percent of the invitees responded. Can you imagine a huge line of doctors waiting to get their teddy bears?

Select a usable, functional item.   Functionality gives the receiver a reason for keeping your gift handy. It works, and that's its reason for being. It doesn't exist solely for self-aggrandizement. I use a pocket shoe polisher as a giveaway. Because I stress the importance of well-shined shoes at trade shows, this is a natural for me. It is functional, and people really like it. In fact, it's so well liked that I get calls for replacements!

Present the gift politely.   Forcing a gift on someone defeats its purpose. Respect your attendees, even if they refuse your trinket.

Not one of these 10 tips is the ultimate answer for every problem. But the more of them that can logically be built into the marketing tool used, the better the probability that it will be kept. And that's the name of the game.

Local Media

Many companies run ads in the business sections of local newspapers a day or two before the show opens. Be careful to weigh the pros and cons of this idea before you commit to it, however. Trade show visitors travel greater distances than most companies think. A survey of regional and national shows revealed that 64 percent of all visitors traveled more than 200 miles to the show.

More and more large trade shows are broadcasting reports in convention hotels via cable TV. They often offer advertising at a fairly reasonable cost. Unfortunately, they probably broadcast mostly to empty rooms. If people are in town to attend the show, why would they be in their hotel rooms?

Other Promotions to Consider

There are many other ways to advertise your presence at an upcoming trade show, and you may certainly consider them as possibilities in your ad campaign. However, let the buyer beware! For one reason or another, most of these methods usually aren't recommended.

Billboards

At large national and international shows some companies use billboards to advertise booth location. Unfortunately, there isn't any way to quantify a return on this investment. It is simply brand-awareness advertising. Also, a billboard reaches everybody who drives by, not just your target market. Don't put your money into billboards, no matter how big you are. There are many more quantifiable ways of using your trade show promotion dollar.

Visitor's Guides

These are specialized guides distributed at trade shows that provide information on where to go and what to do in the convention city. The main problem with these is the same as with the trade publication's show issue. They are passed out during the show—too late! Remember, you want to be on the prospects' appointment calendars *before* they arrive at the show.

Wraparounds

Some magazines and newspapers design a promotional piece to look like their cover which they "wraparound" an issue. Because most attendees stay at one or two hotels, you can arrange for special delivery of these issues to their rooms. This is an eye-catching and tactical promotion, although there are three drawbacks. First, all the attendees at these hotels, whether they are your prospects or not, will get an issue. Second, they're distributed at the show—probably too late. Third, it can be expensive.

There is a way to offset the first two drawbacks, and some magazine publishers will comply with you on it. Have the wraparound designed several months in advance, then send the publisher the names and addresses of your target list. The publisher then sends your "special issue" out with the regular mailing.

Stuffers

A must. Design and print an inexpensive flyer announcing the show, its dates, your location, and what you'll be displaying. Starting three months before the show, include it in every piece of mail (invoices, statements, letters, shipments, *etc.*) that leaves your company.

Other Promotional Tools

The following are powerful yet often overlooked tools. Most small businesses don't even attempt them, but they're actually quite simple. You can do it yourself, too.

Newsletters

A newsletter is a great way to announce your trade show participation. Your customers and prospects already expect it each quarter (or whenever). Prominently display the announcement and be sure to include the name and telephone number of a knowledgeable contact in your company.

Press Releases

The purpose of a press release is to communicate newsworthy information effectively. The content varies. It may encompass, but isn't limited to, news about a new product, an improvement on an existing product, an industry breakthrough, new applications for current products, or personnel changes. The key thing to remember about a press release is that it is not supposed to be an advertisement. Write it like a news story. Give all the pertinent information—who, what, where, when, why, and how—in the first paragraph. Then detail all other features and benefits.

A good press release is one page long, double spaced; it's short. At the top of the page, type *For Immediate Release,* or *For Release on* _____ (whatever date is applicable). Then write the headline and story. At the bottom of the page, add *For further information, contact:* _____ and provide your name, address, and phone number. An editor may want to contact you for more information in order to write an in-depth story. If a photo is available and applicable, include a sharp, five-by-seven, black-and-white print.

Send the release to all publications at least three to four months prior to when you want it published. That's how far ahead magazines work on editorial content. Newspapers work on a much shorter time frame. Just a couple of weeks should be sufficient for them.

Not all publications will use your releases. But if you get one or two printed, it's worth it.

Magazines

If you are an advertiser or potential advertiser, magazines will often write about your company, your products, and you. Although this practice is not recorded in any publishers' corporate policy statements, and many of them would vehemently deny it, the fact is, publishers stay in business by keeping their clients happy. Publishers can provide additional publicity at no cost to the advertiser. The magazine is going to have editorial pages, anyway; they might as well be used to promote advertisers (and their egos). Go ahead and ask for free publicity. Ask for it just before you sign the contract. The worst they can say is no; but the odds are you will receive some good articles.

If you're not an advertiser, or if you run into one of those magazines whose salespeople don't talk with editorial people, you can still get publicity. Give a magazine a good reason to run your story. When talking to an editor, look for an angle that will appeal to the magazine's readership. Don't just suggest they write about you. Offer some unique information about your trade. Editors aren't in the business of giving away free publicity; they're in the information dissemination business: new trends, new breakthroughs in the industry. Give them something relevant to write about, and they'll do so.

Sometimes editors will tell you what type of story they are look-ing for. They know the audience. Give them a story they'll be eager to print. An editor of a large trade publication told me that 80 per-cent of his ideas for stories come from outside sources. Help make the editor's job easier and get some publicity in the process.

Seminars

Surveys have shown that one of the strongest attractions of trade shows is the educational sessions. By participating in these, you are simulta-neously exposed to more prospects and perceived as an expert.

Think about what expertise you have that might be useful to the attendees, then contact the show management and offer your ser-vices as a speaker. Ask what types of programs they look for or what the theme of the upcoming show is. You can then custom design a program for them or volunteer for specific panel discussions. Be sure to do this 9 to 12 months in advance of the show, since that's usu-ally how far in advance they plan.

Although it's not always easy to be placed on the program list, it is possible. And once you've been selected, publicity follows. Not only are you able to capitalize on your presentation by promoting it through your own direct mail campaign, but the show will promote it, too. And, of course, trade publications should also be interested in doing a follow-up story on the "expert."

Be Unique!

It's important to remember that all preshow marketing plans should be designed with your specific show objectives in mind. Regardless of whether your objectives include sales, new leads, public relations, or product research, you want attendees to visit your exhibit. Be cre-ative in your tactics. The following are some ideas to stimulate your creative juices.

Show Badges

For instance, if the show offers preregistration through the mail, why not offer to handle it for your customers and prospects? Arrange for all the badges and then mail them to customers and prospects with an invitation to visit your booth. You can drop a subtle, "Hey, look what we did for you, now you can do this for us." They'll stop by.

Arrange for a Block of Hotel Rooms

As another example, consider what a client of mine in Las Vegas has been doing for years during the Winter Consumer Electronics Show. Each year he sets aside a block of 50 rooms at one of the major hotels. He then offers these rooms as well as airport pickup service to top customers. The customer still pays for the room, but doesn't have to hassle with reservations or taxis. Some customers even joke that they do business with my client just so they will have a room in Las Vegas each year! (An additional benefit from this is knowing where your top customers are staying during the show.)

Trade Show Appointment Book

Pocket planners for prospects to use for scheduling appointments during the show are always welcome. Send them out about four to six weeks before the show. Be clever and fill in one of the time slots for a visit to your booth; they'll get a kick out of it and be there at the appointed time. If they can't make the appointment, they usually call to arrange another time. This planner can also be a great way to promote your products or services through photos and "ads."

Hold a Golf Tournament the Day
Before the Show

Keep in mind, too, that it's not unusual for attendees to mix a little pleasure with business, especially if the show site is nice. One company I know in Southern California arranges a round of golf at one of the top local courses the day before the show opens. They turn it into a small tournament, and bring in a PGA tour player to mingle with the guests. The customers and prospects pay their own way for one extra day and have the time of their lives. Very little business is handled on the course, but every one of those attendees makes an appointment to visit the exhibit during the show.

Trade a Book for an Appointment

Perhaps you've written a book? One author I know, whose company exhibits at many shows, offers an autographed copy of his book to everyone who visits the exhibit. People walk away with something they'll keep, and he walks away with a lot of leads.

Close Your Booth

Finally, take note that for the last couple of years at the Super Show, Nike has closed its booth on the first day of the show and invited its 700 closest friends for a private showing of new products. This is at a show that attracts 100,000 attendees!

Think of the impact this strategy has. To the 700 invitees, Nike is saying, "You're special. In fact, you're so special, we're inviting you to be among the elite few who get to see our new products first!" Imagine how those 700 people feel. Do you think they plan to continue buying from Nike?

And how about the rest of the show attendees? First of all, they want to get in there the second day of the show and see what everybody else saw. And secondly, they're thinking, "I'm going to be on that invited list *next* year."

You might want to close your booth because you have a limited number of prospects attending the show and you want to keep everybody else out. At a recent WESTEC show, one small exhibitor cordoned off its exhibit and only targeted the 60 buyers who qualified for its target market. This allowed the exhibitor to stay focused exclusively on these buyers.

Other Examples:

- At one COMDEX, Microsoft arranged for every hotel room in Las Vegas to have a silk-screened pillowcase put on the pillow. When the exposition guests pulled back the bedcovers that night, they saw the Microsoft logo and booth number.
- Too expensive, you say? The next year, Microsoft made a unique offer to the local cab drivers. When someone got in a cab, the driver was supposed to ask, "Have you been to the Microsoft exhibit yet?" If the cab's customer was one of the top managers from

Microsoft, he or she handed the driver a $500 bill on the spot. Guess how many people were asked *that* question during COMDEX? The whole promotion cost less than $5,000.

- Shortly after Jack Nicklaus won the Masters Championship, one of the divisions of Emerson Electric was preparing for a show. The division was keenly interested in 50 key buyers, who all happened to be golfers. Nicklaus had won the Masters with a special over-size putter, so Emerson sent duplicate putters to the top 50 targets in three separate mailings. The first box had the grip. The second, the shaft. The third, the putter's head. Included in the third box was a note saying, "Stop by the Emerson booth and we'll put it all together for you!" Forty-eight showed up.

- At the International Manufacturing Technology Show, Allen-Bradley invited its top prospects and best customers for a night of billiards at an upscale pool hall in Chicago. The company also hired Don Feeney, a billiards expert, to share tips and promote its products.

- Empire Communications sent a video of customer testimonials in a toxic waste disposal bag obtained from a local military surplus store. The video was accompanied by a letter inviting prospects to visit its exhibit with the message, "Warning—this information may be *toxic* to your competitors."

- Preparing for the Supermarket Industry Convention, Coca-Cola sent out oversized cardboard cutouts of its new contoured can to its top 700 customers. The top of the can had a fliptop, which when pulled up, activated a tiny audio player sounding like a can opening.

- For the American Society of Training & Development Show, Gap International sent out live tree seedlings to targeted prospects, with the message, "We'll help you *grow* your business."

- To separate itself from the hospitality suite clutter at a banking industry exposition, Scopus Inc. held a "Party After the Party" for invited guests. The party was held at a local private club in a quiet setting, featuring after-dinner drinks and cigars.

- At the National Infomercial Marketing Association trade show, Williams Worldwide arranged with the main hotels to leave small boxes of Godiva Chocolates on attendees' pillows (with a message from Williams Worldwide, of course).

- At a computer show, Live Pix set up a mock stunt stage, where attendees could have their pictures taken looking like they were doing a major movie stunt.

- Talk about a culture clash. Anheuser-Busch had Carmen Electra signing posters in its Supermarket Industry Convention exhibit, right next door to the Kraft booth with Regis Philbin.
- M&M Mars brought in the NASCAR stock car it sponsors for attendees to sit in.
- IntelliData had one-sheet floor plans delivered to prospects' rooms at the Retail Delivery '97 trade show. If you brought that flyer with you to its booth, you received a free pair of boxer shorts.
- Several convention and visitors bureaus from different cities in South Carolina banded together to help promote the state. They each sent out a mailing to the preregistered attendee list with one piece of a puzzle. If you brought all the pieces into their co-located booths, you'd be registered for a drawing for a free trip.
- For the All Candy Expo, Bob's Candy Company sent a wave mail campaign of three postcards. Each 5 by 7 card featured bright red and white stripes, like the company's candy canes, with a mystery message to "Come and Get Striped!" The theme was carried throughout its exhibit—in the exhibit design, the uniforms, and the hats the staff gave to visitors who mentioned the mailings.

Where Do You Get Promotion Ideas?

First off, you need to understand where *not* to get ideas. Do *not* look at your fellow exhibitors in the shows you're currently doing or plan to do. Unfortunately, this is all too common. Think about the last show you went to. How many exhibitors gave away bags? If more than one exhibitor is handing out bags, or popcorn, or bottles of water, or keychains, do you remember any of them?

As emphasized throughout this book, it's critical you totally stand out from the crowd. I recommend you follow the advice of two very smart, yet very different men—W. Edwards Deming, father of total quality management (TQM), and Jerry Garcia, of the Grateful Dead.

Deming made it clear in his teachings that benchmarking was a cornerstone of the entire TQM concept. Benchmarking, according to Deming, was the "act of observing correct behavior and then emulating within your own context." He stressed that true benchmarking went far beyond just watching the best players within your own industry. In fact, Deming was critical of companies that limited their studies to their own markets.

By watching and emulating only other companies that do what you do, you are falling into two traps. The first is the trap of following the leader. By emulating your competition, you'll never get better than them. And the second trap is that you'll only *commoditize* what you both produce. Everybody ends up looking alike and acting alike.

Jerry Garcia's Grateful Dead were the world's top money-making band for several years before he died. Yet they rarely produced a new album. Most of their income came from the steady string of concerts they gave to their devoted "deadheads."

Garcia once said, "You don't want to be considered merely the best of the best. You want to be the *only* ones who do what you do."

But where do you get new ideas? Actually, the answer is all around you.

Check Out Other Trade Shows

Are you in the computer/high tech industry? Then attend some shows in totally different industries—food shows, sporting goods shows, medical shows, home shows, boat shows. What do you see that's fairly common at those shows that's not at yours? Working with an exhibitor for the Kitchen & Bath Show, we decided to add a video wall with demos of its products. We got the idea from the Consumer Electronics Show, where *everybody* has a video wall. But nobody had one at the Kitchen & Bath Show. (Well, at least for that first year. The next year there were *six* video walls.)

Spend Time at Your Local Mall

What's a major mall anyway? It's just a permanent trade show that's open to the public.

Walk through the mall with new eyes. Look at the stores as if they were an exhibit. What do they do to draw you in? What catches your eye? Look at the ads in your local newspaper and see how they get you to hop in your car and head down to the mall.

Visit Las Vegas or Atlantic City

Who does a better job of promoting themselves than Vegas? What can you learn just by observing? Walk the strip in Vegas and see how the casinos pull you in. Walk through the casinos and see how they pull you into their games. What incentives and goodies do they offer to entice you?

Be Like Disney World

Take a long look at Disney. Its marketing experts hit you from all sides—TV, movies, radio, merchandise, promotional tie-ins with McDonald's—and that's *before* you get to their theme parks! When you fly into Orlando, they start "Disneyizing" you the moment you get off the plane. The tram ride to baggage claim is narrated by the same voice you hear throughout the Magic Kingdom. When you walk through Disney World, Epcot, Pleasure Island, Animal Kingdom, or any of their other properties, you are hit from all sides. Even while standing in line for an attraction (they don't call them rides), you are entertained and encouraged to have fun and *spend money*.

Also, look at how Disney promotes an upcoming movie. By the time it comes out, you've been immersed in its story, toys, and characters. Sort of like preparing for a trade show? Wouldn't you like attendees to have your company name on their lips when they arrive at the convention center?

Walk Through Your Local Supermarket

Again, like a mall, these are just trade shows in different form. You've got aisles of merchandise, all screaming for your attention. Companies get you with eye-catching shapes and colors. What new ideas can you get from all this? Getting ready for a construction industry trade show, one company found rock candy at its supermarket. A natural tie-in, don't you think?

Other Sources

Your sources for new ideas are all around you. You just have to open your eyes and look for them. The next time you go through your mail, ask yourself what catches your attention and why? How can you borrow that idea and emulate it within your trade show promotions?

Summary

Let's face it: preshow marketing is important. The sad thing is that most companies do very little. Remember the Management Mirage. Plan an *effective* preshow campaign that will draw hundreds of qualified buyers to your exhibit. Many companies that say they use preshow marketing really don't—sending out those preprinted registration flyers from show management is not effective. Telling buyers, in casual conversation, to "drop by sometime during the show" is not effective. Sending a memo to all your reps two weeks before the show imploring them to bring their key prospects by the booth is not effective.

Those companies that understand they are responsible for the success of their show make a dedicated commitment to effective preshow marketing. This commitment ensures their success.

CHAPTER 5

At the Show

Getting Set

Effective preshow planning and marketing need to be reinforced by a solid effort at the show. Last-minute problems do occur, but there are a number of ways to alleviate them.

Early Arrival

The show opens tomorrow; to save money, you've decided to fly the show staff in tonight. They can set up early Thursday morning.

Although this is a common practice, it is risky. Major problems can occur. Trade shows are highly stressful situations. It's been rumored that Murphy's Law was named after an ex–exhibit manager. Believe me—if something can go wrong, it will. Exhibits don't arrive on time. Products disappear. Literature is misrouted. The labor you hired never shows up. The carpet is the wrong color. Another company is in your booth space (it's happened to me). Flights are delayed, or worse, canceled. The show doesn't have much of a chance of success if you, your people, or your equipment isn't there on time, or at all. If any of these situations arise and you don't have the time to correct them—well, you're out of luck. The show will go on without you.

That's why I recommend arriving no later than two days before the show begins. Always have your booth ready 24 hours prior to the show's opening. There are two major reasons for these recommendations. First, the exhibit will be ready. After all, isn't that what you're going to the show for in the first place? By setting up the day before, you give yourself enough time to handle last-minute, unexpected emergencies. Second, you have allowed yourself plenty of time to go through final briefings.

In addition, if your exhibit requires outside help in being set up, be sure to coordinate this with your transportation people and show labor. Know when the exhibit is going to arrive at the show site and plan to set up as soon as possible. By arranging this with the labor service ahead of time, you'll avoid potential headaches and conflicts. The best situation is to have your booth delivered and erected on the first day the show site is available.

Such forethought ensures that you will be ready for the show. By having your exhibit ready 24 hours ahead of time, you'll be able to prepare for the upcoming carnival. Trade shows are mentally and physically exhausting. So get a good night's sleep the night before the show. You'll feel fresher, less stressed out, and more alert.

Order Services in Advance

Even if it doesn't seem fair that you have to send your money in far ahead of time to get a discount on services, do it anyway. Your main concern should be getting the job done right, and on time. If you wait to arrange services until you arrive at the show site, you'll have waited too long. You have to stand in several different lines to order the various services you require. Then you have to wait in your booth for the services or rentals to arrive. Often, you sit in your booth and wait . . . and wait . . . and wait; sometimes these things take hours. Do you really need to go through all that?

Another benefit of preordering is that the service companies can efficiently plan on providing you with their services. By giving them advance notice, the odds are you'll arrive at the show and find your electricity, telephone, carpet, and other services all ready for you. That reduces stress.

Other Considerations

Some rules and regulations may affect your booth or show performance. Be sure to read them thoroughly and discuss any problems with show management. The kit will also contain the paperwork for the services you order in advance. Of course, if you've put together the Exhibit Planning Handbook, outlined in Chapter 3, you'll have all this.

And remember, you'll need money. You may have missed something in preparing for the show—you may need to order some things from show services or buy forgotten supplies from the local store. Furthermore, tips may or may not be necessary for services rendered. It's a good idea to be ready, regardless.

Showtime: Two Scenarios

Do you remember the first time you attended a major, national show and walked into the hall before the show opened? It probably resembled chaos in a concrete jungle. People were all over the place. Union laborers were puzzling over exhibit plans. Telephone installers were cherrypicking in the girders high overhead. Forklifts were speeding up and down aisles stacked with crates, cartons, and rolls of carpet. It seemed as if there were no way the show could be ready to open on time.

That's certainly the way it always seems. But somehow, magically, on the first morning of the show, everything falls into place. Forklifts and laborers fade away; carpets appear in the aisles; electricity is turned on and the hall shines. Almost miraculously, the show opens on time.

As it turns out, everybody involved in show preparation had a special job to do. Every laborer, installer, floor manager, union supervisor, and exhibit manager played an important role in getting the show ready on time.

Show preparation includes you, too. You have to make sure everything in your exhibit is in place when the doors open—exhibit up, signage and graphics up, products out, personnel ready, crates and cartons properly stored, and booth clean. As the adage has it: You have two ways of getting all this accomplished—you can do it the hard way, or you can do it the easy way.

The Horror Show

Because you live just 100 miles away from the show, you don't send your exhibit ahead of time; you plan to bring it in your car. You haven't ordered any services for the show, although you're going to need quite a few: electricity, a telephone, a sign for the booth, some chairs and tables (draped), a carpet, daily booth cleaning, a security cage, and a model to pass out literature. The show doesn't open until 1:00 P.M., so you plan to drive in that morning to set up, which you also plan to do yourself.

You arrive at the show site at 8:00 A.M., assuming you have plenty of time to set up. First, you need a dolly to get your booth inside because it's too large to carry, plus you have a lot of samples and literature. But nobody will loan you a dolly or even a handcart; all those union guys seem to be permanently attached to one and not about to let go. After a frustrating hour of looking (it's 9:00) and begging ("Please, pal, I only need it for 10 minutes!"), you finally relent and go to the service desk for help. You stand in line for 18 minutes (9:18). The person behind the desk tells you to wait close by, so there you stand twiddling your thumbs. Another 22 minutes go by (9:40) before someone with a dolly is located. He follows you to your car and, with your help, loads everything onto the dolly and takes it to your booth. He moves fast and takes only 38 more minutes of your time (10:18).

After parking your car, you go to your booth and realize you can't set up without putting the carpet down first. You hike back to the service desk and again stand in line. This time it takes only 11 minutes to get your carpet ordered and go back to your booth (10:29). You're finally settling down from the minor panic of searching for a handcart. You figure you still have plenty of time before the show opens. To kill some time, though, you start to open some of your product and literature boxes.

Twenty minutes go by (10:49) and you're getting a little antsy because the carpet hasn't arrived yet. Another 16 minutes pass (11:05) and you start thinking you could have ordered the electricity, telephone, chairs and tables, model, security cage, and cleaning if you had known it was going to take so long to get a lousy carpet. Finally the carpet arrives and is rolled out in 1 minute (11:06). You immediately begin unpacking your booth to set up. You get the framework put up when you remember you still need to order the rest of your services. You look at your watch and see that it's now 11:23. You realize you only have 1 hour and 37 minutes before the show opens and the panic begins to set in. You race off to the service desks. Nearing them, you realize that every one of them—electricity, telephone, chairs and tables, models, security cages, and cleaning—has a separate desk. You've got to stand in every one of those lines! It's 11:26. You begin to sweat. The first line (electricity) isn't so bad, only 9 minutes (11:35). The next (telephone) is good, too; only 8 minutes (11:43). But you're getting more and more nervous, and you still have four more desks to visit. There are at least 10 people in line ahead of you at the furniture rental desk. The line barely crawls. Five minutes go by, then 10, 15, 20! One by achingly slow one the line gets shorter. Twenty-five minutes have passed (12:08). Finally, it's your turn. You place your order, but you almost have a big payment problem. How were you supposed to know that they wouldn't bill you? Fortunately, you had your VISA card to cover it. Luckier still, they took it.

Time is really short now (12:18). You realize there is no way to get the other three services (model, security cage, and cleaning) and still have time to finish setting and cleaning up in time for the opening. You decide you don't really need cleaning, that you can do it yourself. The model is also canceled because she was only going to pass out literature anyway. And, since you've never been ripped off before, you decide to hide your samples in boxes underneath the tables.

By now you're a nervous wreck. You run back to your booth and find the union supervisor waiting for you. He politely explains to you about the unwritten "Half-Hour Rule": It seems that, unless you can put up your exhibit in less than 30 minutes, you must use qualified union help. He points out that you started setting up at 11:06. You turn white and start to plead; it works this time. After eliciting a promise that you'll never, ever set up or tear down your booth without union help, he lets you off the hook with a warning. It's now 12:31 P.M.

Shifting into high gear, you throw the rest of your booth together and pull out your products for display. As the magic hour of 1:00 passes, you're still setting out brochures and plugging in lights. Buyers start to roam through the aisles, but they see you're not set up and leave you alone. The chairs and table arrive at 1:30. The table drape arrives at 1:50. You still haven't cleaned up or put on a tie.

By 2:10, things in the booth are in order. Now you can go to the rest room and get dressed. But you don't have a model; if you leave your booth, it'll be unmanned. So you ask the person in the booth next door to keep an eye out. Finally, by 2:43, you're dressed and the booth looks passable. But the events of the last 6 hours and 43 minutes have left you frazzled, both mentally and physically. You can't wait till the show closes at 6:00. Unfortunately, that attitude shows and carries over to the rest of the show, which is a failure.

Is this any way to work at a trade show? Of course not. Was this scenario a farfetched nightmare, completely unrealistic? Unfortunately, no. It's surprising how many times over the years I've witnessed such scenes.

The Dream Show

It's 6:00 A.M. Wednesday morning, and you're packing your clothes. The show is scheduled to open at 1:00 P.M. on Thursday. Because the show site is only 100 miles away, you plan to drive in. That's not a problem because you're getting an early start.

Before loading the car, you go over your trade show handbook one last time. Everything has gone smoothly and well within the time plan. The exhibit was shipped early and you've received confirmation from your carrier's local rep that it arrived at the show safely. All the products for display and literature were packed with the booth, so everything is there. You double-check to see if anything is missing that you'll need: You have an exhibitor's kit, copies of all advance service orders, and enough traveler's checks to take care of any last-minute items. Everything's ready, so you load the car and hit the road by 9:00 A.M.

You arrive at the show site before noon. After parking the car, you head to your booth. The carpet you preordered is already down and everything you shipped is waiting in the booth. The preordered, draped tables, chairs, electricity, security cage, and telephone connection are also in place. You have plenty of time before the labor you ordered arrives at 2:00 to set up, so you head to the service desks to confirm your model and daily cleaning.

Because you've arrived a day ahead of time, there is almost no line, and within 30 minutes you've confirmed both services. During the remaining time, you explore the show site. With your checklist in hand, you find out where the food concessions, rest rooms, first aid booths, security office, fire alarms, and pay telephones are located. After finding these, you head for registration to pick up your show badges and exhibitor guide. On your way back to the booth, you stop by the show office to introduce yourself to the manager.

By now it's nearly 2:00 and time to be at your booth to set up. The labor and supervisor arrive right on time. You knew they would be reliable because you hired them through an established exhibit house. They get right to work erecting the exhibit while you unpack products. It takes most of the afternoon to prepare everything to your satisfaction, but by 5:00 P.M. the booth looks great.

After storing your products in the security cage for overnight safekeeping, you head off to the hotel. You enjoy a relaxing evening and dinner, comfortable in the thought that everything is ready for tomorrow.

The morning comes. Because the show doesn't open till 1:00, you have time to take care of a number of phone calls and see one of your local clients for a short time. You arrive at the show by 11:00 to set out all your products and store the security cage behind your booth. Because of its overnight cleaning, the booth is ready to go.

At 12:15, the model you hired arrives and you go over her responsibilities. By 12:45, you're all set. You're fresh, excited, and anxious for the show to begin. At 1:00 P.M., the show opens and you attract the first buyers into your booth and convert them into qualified prospects. The show becomes an unqualified success.

Does this sound like a pipe dream? Well, it's not. Can things really run this smoothly during installation and setup? The answer is a resounding yes! By following the simple steps I've outlined on planning ahead, you will be ready to go when the show begins.

Presenting Your Products

There are three parts of a trade show that determine your success. All three are equally important. First is the booth itself. Second is the personnel staffing the booth. And third is the product or service you are selling. (Hereafter, in this section, when I refer to *product,* it means product or service.)

What your product is or what it does is not important here. But there are four matters associated with your product that are important to the success of your trade show. And you have control over all four.

Product Knowledge

This sounds like a lesson from "Business 101," but it's amazing to me—and to the buyers I've talked to—just how little people know about the product they're selling. In fact, 70 percent of buyers surveyed stated that their biggest complaint about booth personnel was lack of product knowledge.[1]

To illustrate just how important product knowledge is, I'll relate a story about a large, international corporation. Every year it would bring together its top salespeople from around the world for a few days of rest and relaxation as a reward for their contributions. The guest of honor was that year's top producer, and he or she would be feted at the last night's banquet and would give the keynote address.

When the time came for the speech, everyone pulled out pens and paper to write down the pearls of wisdom the "top gun" would present. Everyone in the audience aspired to be there and didn't want to miss a trick.

[1]*The Adventure of Trade Shows,* 1997.

As the story goes, one year the honoree, after being introduced, rose slowly and walked to the front amidst a standing ovation. He placed his hands on the podium and looked around the room. His eyes surveyed his surroundings. He remained silent while the people sat down. After the room quieted, he continued to look around. Finally, after several seconds of uncomfortable silence, he began his speech. He said, "I defy anybody in this room to ask me a question about our products that I can't answer." With that, he ended his talk, walked back to his chair, and sat down.

Know your product. It pays.

Product Demonstration

If your product can be demonstrated, be prepared to do so. Prospects will better understand and appreciate your products if shown how they work. Too often at trade shows the booth staff doesn't understand how to operate products. Prospects will most certainly be turned off by this. After all, if you can't show how your own product works, how can they be expected to operate it?

The key to successful demonstration can be summed up in three words: practice, practice, practice. The more you practice demonstrating your product, the better you'll be able to show it off at the show. The more you understand its different capabilities and how they work, the more you'll be able to show each prospect how your product will work for him or her.

The worst time to learn how to demonstrate is the morning of the first day. There is too much going on around you to learn properly, and, frankly, it's too late. Make sure you know how to operate and demonstrate your product before you leave for the show. In addition, if you are in charge of the show, make sure your booth staff members all know, too. Hold a training session at least the day before the show opens to review product demonstrations and floor selling techniques (more on that later in this chapter).

A critical element in demonstration is the product itself. Make sure it works! A product demonstration with a product that doesn't work or perform to expectations is a sure mark of unprofessionalism. The prospect will be unimpressed or, more likely, uninterested.

Each morning before the show opens, go through a trial demo with your product. Don't just turn it on to see if the lights work; put it through all the paces required for a normal demonstration. Then, if anything goes wrong, you can fix it by show time. Things do occasionally go wrong. It's a fact of life that products, no matter how durable, can break down. As an extra precaution, bring at least one backup unit. That way, if something does go wrong, you can quickly direct the prospect to the second model.

Compare Your Product to the Competition's

Trade shows, as I've pointed out earlier, are like shopping malls; attendees can comparison shop among companies. If you make a specific comparison between your product and that of a competitor, it's a simple task for the prospect to walk down the aisle and verify your claim. Thus, it's important for you to know exactly how you stand with the competition. What new products are they showing? What's their pricing structure? What kind of terms are they offering? How soon are they able to fill orders? What advantages does your product have over theirs? What advantages does their product have over yours? How can you overcome those disadvantages?

As Sun Tzu says in the book *The Art of War* (New York: Delacorte Press, 1983):

> If you know the enemy and yourself, you need not fear the result of a hundred battles. If you know yourself but not the enemy, for every victory gained you will also suffer a defeat. If you know neither the enemy nor yourself, you will succumb in every battle.

That book is 2,500 years old and was written for military strategists. But its words are just as important in today's battlefield of business.

Product Enthusiasm

Product enthusiasm sounds corny, but it's vital. Enthusiasm and excitement are catching. I've seen salespeople at shows act bored and even apologetic about their products in front of attendees. Why are they at the show? Why do they even work for that company? If you aren't enthusiastic about your own product, can you expect anybody else to be?

Ongoing Training

A Personal Story

Several years ago, I was working as a sales rep for Technicolor's VCR division. I was in my 20s and was the youngest and greenest of the 30 or so salespeople. One January we prepared for the Winter Consumer Electronics Show in Las Vegas. The day before the show opened, Technicolor held a staff meeting. The purpose of the meeting was to educate us all on the newest products on display at the show and motivate us for successful floor selling. The vice president for sales gave a thorough presentation, carefully explaining all the features and benefits of our entire product line. In a classroom-style setup, we listened to his lecture. A few people, including me, took notes. Most didn't.

After the product presentation, the president of the corporation walked to the front of the room and introduced a motivational speaker. This man came forward and proceeded to try to motivate us. He talked about how sales was an exciting profession, how we could provide "warm fuzzies" for our customers, how our opportunities for success were unlimited. Needless to say, it didn't work. Despite the fact Technicolor had one of the most innovative product lines in the industry, the show was a disaster. Very few orders were written, and, worse, very few qualified prospects emerged from the thousands who poured into the booth.

Of those few orders, most were written by me. Yet, I certainly wasn't some sort of *wunderkind* salesperson. I had not yet shown any special talent for selling. In fact, less than five years earlier, I had been told by another sales manager to get out of sales because I didn't have the aptitude for it. I wasn't responsible for a large geographic region for Technicolor. In fact, my territory wasn't geographic at all. It was called "special markets"—mail order and premium/incentive. Both are notorious for the amount of time typically required for closing deals. And I wasn't a particularly aggressive salesperson, either. In fact, at that time in my career, I wasn't even sure I wanted to be a salesperson. I was intimidated by the whole business.

But, the fact is, I did have a successful show, more so than any other salesperson working the Technicolor booth. Why? After all, I attended the same so-called training session with all the other salespeople. What did I learn that nobody else learned? Was I just lucky, or did I have some special, inside knowledge?

In a way, I did have such knowledge. First, I had already heard the story about the salesperson of the year and his product knowledge. And, whether it was true or not, it made an impression on me. For weeks before the show, I learned everything I could about the Technicolor product line, studying every available piece of material. I asked Technicolor engineers as many questions as I could. I learned how to operate all the Technicolor products until I could demonstrate them as well as the people who designed them. I learned all about the advantages we had over the competition. In short, I knew our product line cold. I was prepared to answer almost any question a prospect could ask of me.

In addition, I had the benefit of some private tutoring: from my father. Having participated in every Consumer Electronics Show since its inception, he taught himself how to work a trade show. He taught me how to dress, how to assume a correct posture, how to project a positive image, how to approach attendees, and how to qualify prospects.

With all that knowledge and training, it was no wonder that I was probably the most enthusiastic salesperson in that booth. I was totally sold on the Technicolor line. I was eager to meet attendees. I helped other salespeople with questions and demonstrations. My enthusiasm was contagious to my customers, and, because of all that, I had a successful show.

The point of this story is not my diligence. The fact is, Technicolor's vcr division went out of business soon after. The point is, proper training and education are fundamental to the success of your show. Many companies hold meetings before trade shows, and a few even incorporate some training. But *proper* training makes the difference.

As I've stated before, trade shows are demanding. You can't just go to a show, put up your booth, set out your products, hang the corporate logo, and sit back waiting for people to flock to your exhibit. In bad English, it ain't gonna happen. Making sure your booth staff knows that your product line is critical. Training them on the ins and outs of your products or services is a must before any show. Don't wait until it's too late—do it before everyone leaves for the show. Give everybody a full day's hands-on training at your facility. Let them talk to your engineers or designers or developers. The more they learn through actual, experiential training and interaction, the more they'll remember.

Preshow Training Ideas

If it's just not feasible to bring the entire staff to your location, send them as much information as possible. Of course, we all know how difficult it is to make people study independently, so here are a few ideas that may help.

Audiotapes.   Produce audiotapes on product information and training for trade shows. Your staff can listen to them while traveling. Many people learn more through listening rather than reading, anyway. It's also an effective attention-getter.

Newsletters.   A monthly product newsletter is a creative way of providing information. It could be written in a newsy, easy-to-read style, with catchy headlines.

Incentives.   Build an incentive for learning. Send out the information along with a quiz. Anybody answering all the questions correctly gets a prize or bonus.

Contests.   Create your own "Mystery Prospect" contest for the upcoming trade show. Tell everyone that there will be several planted attendees at the show who will judge each salesperson on his or her presentation. At the end of the show, the one judged to have given the best presentation wins a major prize.

Regardless of such efforts, it's still important to have a meeting just prior to the show, for two reasons: first, to explain clearly to all staff members what the company's trade show objectives are and what their role is in achieving each one of them; second, to show them how to accomplish these objectives. The first should have been established before the show; now you must establish individual responsibilities. Let's look at an example of how this might work:

> Your company is planning to exhibit at this year's Supermarket Industry Convention in Chicago. The show will be open three days for a total of 19 hours. Through careful analysis (and help from the formulas in Chapter 2), you plan to rent a 10-foot by 20-foot in-line booth, a total of 200 square feet. You know the exhibit will take up 60 square feet, leaving you 140 square feet for your people. Knowing that you need approximately 50 square feet per salesperson, you decide on three

salespersons (140/50 = 2.8 people [round up to 3]). With three people on duty at all times, averaging six contacts per hour each, you achieve 18 contacts per hour. By multiplying the number of contacts per hour by total show hours, you get your total show objective:

18 contacts/hour × 19 hours = 342 contacts

Of course, you know that in order to have the most efficient booth staff, you'll need to rotate two shifts of salespeople. That means you'll need six salespeople, each working a total of nine and a half hours at the show. By dividing the projected number of contacts equally among the six salespeople, you'll get their individual objectives:

342 contacts ÷ 6 = 57 contacts each

You can now tell your salespeople that each one has an objective of 57 contacts at the show.

Note: Keep in mind that this is only one way of setting quantifiable show objectives. This particular method only counts show contacts. It doesn't necessarily mean *qualified* contacts.

By calculating corporate objectives in this manner, you establish a way of measuring your progress at the end of each day.

Note: Don't limit yourself to just one meeting before the show. Have a short, daily meeting after the show closes. This way you can find out on the spot how everybody did that day in comparison to his or her goals. In addition, you can share any new information that may be helpful tomorrow; for example, significant new trends, industry announcements, competitor reports, and so forth.

If you really want to stay on top, have a short meeting after every shift comes off the floor. Tally total contacts and give on-the-spot awards to the people who got the most leads.

Factors in Trade Show Success

Once you've clearly stated what is expected of everyone, you can move on to the second part of your preshow meeting—how to accomplish these objectives. Although we'll go into greater detail on boothmanship in Chapter 6, there are a number of other factors to be considered.

A trade show is not a holiday!   In the 1992 Trade Show Bureau's (Center for Exhibition Industry Research) Simmons Study, prospects were asked why they attended a trade show.[2] The top reasons given included:

- 77% look for information on the latest styles and trends in their industry
- 73% look for information on the latest technology in their industry
- 72% look for information on where to purchase or order a product
- 61% look for information about products and services from companies around the United States
- 51% look for information that helps evaluate specific products or services

No one in that study stated "vacation" as a reason for attending a trade show. Unfortunately, too many salespeople treat shows as just that. Although a more relaxed attitude may have prevailed 20 years ago, today's trade show is a fiercely competitive arena.

During training sessions, people often ask me how long one's hours are at a trade show. My answer is simple. When you're awake, you're working. Just because the show hours are 9:00 A.M. to 6:00 P.M. doesn't mean those are the only hours you can be productive. Get together with clients and prospects for breakfast before the show opens; it's a great way to start the day. It is my opinion that you and your salespeople should refrain from all alcoholic beverages during the show week. Alcohol slows the reflexes and dulls the mind when trying to make intelligent and rational decisions. We've all heard the war stories about trade show parties and revelry. Unfortunately, I've heard about more of those episodes destroying sales opportunities and customer relationships than helping to create such relationships. Maybe 20 to 30 years ago drinking and selling worked together, but not anymore. The buyers and your competition are too sophisticated for that now. Don't take the chance.

[2]"The Power of Trade Shows," Simmons Study, 1992 Trade Show Bureau.

There are plenty of people whom you will want to spend more than just 10 minutes with at the show. Buyers are there to work the whole show—take advantage of it! Of course, there's always one other consideration: If your customers and prospects aren't having breakfast or dinner with you, rest assured they're with someone else. Your competition, maybe?

A trade show is not a game! I won a sales contest from my company once. The first prize was an all-expense-paid trip to Frankfurt, West Germany, for the annual Frankfurt Messe, a consumer goods show. Our company exhibited at the show each year, and the big bosses felt that this was an opportunity to reward the best salespeople.

I flew coach class in a crowded plane from Los Angeles to New York and then to Frankfurt. It took nearly 18 hours to get there, and I arrived in Frankfurt at 8:00 A.M., local time. After checking in at my hotel, I had to help set up our exhibit, which took all day. I didn't sleep a wink that night because of the time change. The next morning the show opened—for six days, ten hours a day. Some incentive reward.

I guarantee you that the following year I did not win that sales contest. Don't think you're rewarding your salespeople by offering trade shows as incentives. You're not.

Clean your booth! One of the biggest turnoffs to prospects is a dirty booth. Make everyone responsible for keeping the booth clean. Keep trash cans and ashtrays emptied, even if it must be done every five minutes. A clean booth is a sign of a company that cares about its appearance; it also denotes professionalism.

Define your objectives! I've already gone over this, but it doesn't hurt to emphasize. It's one thing for the corporate management to know what the objectives are, but it won't do any good if the booth staff doesn't know them. Make sure you clearly define what is expected from your staff. Give everybody clearly defined, quantifiable objectives. Also, have each person establish personal objectives.

Stand apart! I used to say that you should dress a notch above everybody else at the show, but not anymore. With hundreds, maybe even thousands, of other exhibitors at a show, you should be looking for every opportunity to separate yourself from the crowd. That includes how you dress. If everybody else is wearing suits (at medical shows, IMTS, or CES, as examples), I want my exhibitors wearing casual attire. If everybody else is wearing casual clothes (*i.e.,* Surf Expo, the PGA Merchandise Show), I would really dress up.

There are three reasons for doing this. First, you'll look different. How can somebody tell your staff from anybody else if you all look alike? Second, it creates a "look" at your booth and offers a team-building opportunity for you. And third, staffers can't use it as a crutch, blending in and hiding with everybody else.

If there is an exception to this rule, it would be shoes. You're on your feet all day, for several days; that's hard on the whole body, as well as tiring. Wear comfortable shoes with soft soles. Several manufacturers these days make comfortable dress shoes. Alternatively, put some new footpads in your dress shoes; they'll make a world of difference. Definitely, do not wear new shoes, looking to break them in. You'll be sorry you did!

Hold the literature!   In my opinion, literature is the biggest and fattest sacred cow in trade shows today. Everybody finds good, logical reasons for continuing to pass out literature. But, in reality, where did this practice originate? From the guy across the aisle at our first show, that's where.

When you hand somebody a piece of literature, where does it initially go? In a bag, right? What else is in that bag? Everybody else's literature! Is that standing out from the crowd or blending in with the crowd?

The fact is, most literature passed out at trade shows doesn't even make it out the front door of the convention center. In addition, a lot of it ends up in the hands of our competition. I don't know about you, but I want to have a lot more control over who gets my information.

Look at it this way. There are three things that a prospect can do with the flyer you give him or her:

1. Walk around the corner and throw it out. This happens a lot. In fact, you could probably restock your supply of flyers at the end of each day just by retrieving them from the trash cans around the corner.
2. Stuff it in a plastic bag and take it back to the hotel room. Then he or she could spend that night culling through the pile to decide which literature will be taken back on the airplane (you didn't think they'd take it all back did you?). Don't expect a prospect to take too much time reading through all the material he or she has collected, maybe three to five seconds per piece.
3. Put it in a briefcase and take it back to the office, just like you want.

Of these three possibilities, the one with the least chance is the third.

As you meet prospects, tell them you'll send the literature after the show. They'll be happier to hear you say that because they won't have to worry about it. It makes you look more professional, and it saves you a lot of wasted money. Be sure you do follow up and send the literature immediately after the show. (More about that in Chapter 8.)

Pounce!   Studies have shown that you have about two to three seconds for every 10 feet of linear space to attract the prospect's attention. Make sure your people are ready for that moment when the attendee shows interest. This is not a time for shyness, hesitation, or inexperience.

No novices!   You certainly wouldn't send a green, inexperienced sales rep to call on a major buyer out in the field. For the same reason, you don't want to have a novice working your booth at a trade show. When an important buyer walks in, you want your best salesperson waiting.

Furthermore, trade shows are no place for sales training. The atmosphere is noisy, crowded, intimidating, and highly charged—hardly conducive for training. If you simply must use trade shows to train your sales staff, do it at small local or regional shows where little harm can be done. You definitely don't want rookies working at your most important show of the year. And, as always, if you wait until the show is open to train people for floor selling, it's too late.

CHAPTER 6

Working with Your Staff

Working the Booth

You know by now that a trade show is no place for sales training. You place your corporate investment in the show at great risk by exhibiting with novice representatives. Your booth staff must be ready for action and alert to every opportunity to further your objectives.

There are as many contrasts between field sales and trade show sales as there are similarities. Let's revisit some of those differences.

In the field, you go to the buyer. At a trade show, they come to you. Just think about it. Buyers from all over the world (or at least from all over your region) might be coming to the show to find answers to their problems, look for new products, and learn about their industry. What an incredible opportunity! Rather than traveling to see them, they are traveling to see you. That's a great advantage.

In the field, you are on their turf. At a trade show, they are on yours. This observation, of course, has much to do with the power game we all play. When you meet at a client's or prospect's office, the client or prospect is in control. There can be quite a few distractions: phone calls, unexpected visitors, a secretary bringing in messages, coffee, or the mail. Although trade shows definitely have distractions, buyers are out of their comfort zone. The distractions don't belong to his/her company; in fact, you can design your booth so that the only distractions buyers see are purposely put there. You control the environment; you can create any atmosphere you want. You hold the power.

The field is not always conducive to demonstrations; a trade show is perfect for them. Earthmovers, for example, are a little bit difficult to get into a prospect's office. You can show lots of shiny 8 by 10 colored glossies backed up with a few dozen testimonials, but there's nothing like a trade show for demonstrations. You can let them climb all over that earthmover. You can set up a real life demonstration at a show; bring in a few tons of dirt and let the *prospect* move it around.

Furthermore, you can develop a multimedia presentation along with the product that will impress your prospects. That's tough to do in somebody's small, private office.

At a trade show, you can see more prospects in one hour than you'll see all week in the field. Trade shows do not require driving around looking for nonexistent addresses. There is no waiting in an impersonal lobby with a dozen other salespeople. Buyers come to you at a trade show, and they come to you *en masse*. As soon as you're done talking to one prospect, along comes another! Depending on your product and marketplace, you can see 6, 10, even 15 prospects every hour. That's a gold mine!

At a trade show, prospects are in a more relaxed, buying mode. They're away from the distractions of the office; it's probably a nice break for them. We all have several responsibilities at the office, and buyers are no exception. They simply don't spend 100 percent of their time buying. They are there for specific reasons—to solve problems, see new technology, visit potential vendors. Their minds are on the show, not back at the office.

At a trade show, you are forced to make a lot of cold calls. Many of us just don't like to make cold calls, and for that reason a lot of time in the field is spent with people we know. Very little time is spent in face-to-face contact with total strangers. At a trade show, contact with lots of strangers is standard. For many of us, that's a very uncomfortable situation, but it's necessary if business is to expand.

It's not unusual to spend a lot of time with prospects in the field, sometimes several hours. Unfortunately, you don't have that luxury at a trade show. There are only a finite number of minutes at a show, and you need to see as many people as possible in that time. Quite often you'll spend as little as 10 minutes with a prospect, and many times much less.

The cost of closing a sale in the field is more than four times as expensive as at a trade show. Every time an industrial salesperson calls on a client, it costs his employer $229.70, according to a study on 1985 costs conducted by the McGraw-Hill Laboratory of Advertising Performance. That same study reported that the average number of sales calls required to close an order was 5.5, a total of $1,263.35.[1] Compare those figures to the Trade Show Bureau's (Center for Exhibition Industry Research) Research Reports Nos. 18 and 2020. Every time a salesperson makes contact with a qualified prospect at a trade show, it costs $106.89. In addition, the average number of follow-up calls needed to close a sale is 0.8, with 54 percent of all leads closed without a personal sales call.[2] Even with the follow-up call, the total of that sale is only $290.65—less than one-fourth the cost in the field!

Of course, there are many other differences, but these certainly give you a good idea about the contrasts. Take note of them; both you and your salespeople must learn how to properly work a trade show exhibit.

Creating a New Relationship

As I've said before, the purpose of business is to create and maintain long-term customer relationships. Before I share the steps you can use to interact with someone at a trade show, it's important to first look at how you begin a new relationship in today's business climate.

In creating a new relationship, eight steps are required:

1. You must *meet* them. Whether you're doing this at a trade show or in their office, you must, at some point, get face-to-face with your prospect.
2. You must *qualify* that person. Any meeting you have, whether out in the field or at a trade show, it's critical that you only meet with people who have a role in the decision-making process. That doesn't mean they are just decision-makers. They could be influencers, specifiers, or even end-users. More and more companies are creating *vertical buying teams,* where several different people are all involved in the

---

[1]McGraw-Hill Lab of Advertising Performance (1985). Specific source is the "Trade Show Bureau Research Report No. 2020," July 1986.

[2]Trade Show Bureau Research Report Nos. 18, April 1983, and 2020, July 1986.

decision-making process. As long as they are part of the loop, you want to talk with them. The way to identify a qualified prospect is discussed later in this chapter.

3. You must develop *rapport* with them. It's an old adage, but true. People do business with people they like. People do business with people they know. And people do business with people they trust. If they don't like you, you can forget about any type of long-term relationship. (And don't fall into the trap of thinking they *have* to buy from you because you've got the only product on the market. They'll buy from you because they have to—until they don't have to.) You can learn more about how to establish rapport later in this chapter.

4. You must *gather information*. In this step, you're looking to learn as much as you can about their company. How long have they been in business? Where are they located? Are they international, national, or regional? How do they currently handle (inventory control, accounting, tool and die switching—whatever problem you're solving)? The purpose of this step is to help you . . .

5. *Uncover* the acknowledged need, problem, or painful situation they have. This is crucial because this provides the connection you have with them. Notice I state "acknowledged need." This is also important. You may think that many companies/people "need" your product or service. But the harsh reality is that not everybody will agree with your thinking.

   For example, I am a marketing consultant, specializing in the trade show industry. I work with corporations (that exhibit at trade shows) to *measurably* impact their overall corporate marketing objectives through exhibiting. I also work with the trade shows themselves to *measurably* impact the value of their show for both exhibitors and attendees. I believe that everybody who exhibits at a trade show or who produces a trade show needs me. However, not everybody agrees with that statement. And that's OK. It is a much harder and more painful process for me to first sell people on acknowledging the need and then sell them on the fact that I am their best solution.

   I should also point out that if you are able to find people who have an acknowledged problem or even a painful situation, you've got a great chance of converting them into new customers. People always want to get rid of a problem, and they will move heaven and earth to get rid of a painful situation.

6. Once you uncover the needs linkage, you then provide a *unique solution* that includes your product and/or service.
7. Knowing they will check out what other alternatives are available to them, you will provide some type of *competitive comparison* information, proving that you have the superior solution.
8. And, finally, if you've done a thorough job of walking through each of these steps, you should be able to reach *mutual agreement.*

You'll notice the difference between this and the old school of selling. It used to be you'd meet someone, make a little small talk, then launch into a pitch for your product or service. Then you'd try a trial close, overcome objections, spar back and forth, fight over the price, and maybe, just maybe, get the sale.

It's unbelievable to me how often I see that type of approach at trade shows. An attendee walks into the booth and the staffer automatically launches into a product pitch, without ever asking any qualifying questions or gathering any information about the attendee's company or needs.

Nobody wants to be sold to that way anymore. We all want personalized, customized relationships. We want to know that the people we send checks to understand our business and care about us personally.

But how much of this relationship building can we accomplish during an encounter that might only last two or three minutes? Not much actually, which is why I've developed the following EQUIP system for trade show encounters.

The EQUIP Concept

What happens during the 5- to 10-minute interaction between an attendee and a salesperson? How can a salesperson properly prepare for this short encounter so as to get the most out of it? The first step is to break the process down and get an overview of what is happening.

As with any meeting in social or business situations, there first needs to be some type of introduction. In a trade show, this would simply be some light conversation with the attendee. Once the conversation has begun, it's important to move quickly into the qualification/presentation step: Who are you talking to? What are his or her needs? How can you help? Once you have covered these steps and the prospect acknowledges the possibility of working with you, then move into the final step—the close. The close is simply asking for action toward your show objective. For example, if your objective is to gather leads for later follow-up, your close would be to get the prospect to commit to a personal call after the show.

I've developed the EQUIP concept to cover each step in the trade show encounter: E stands for entice, Q for qualify, U for uncover, I for introduce, and P for postshow. Let's analyze each of these steps.

Entice

Somewhere along the line, we've developed the impression that exhibit staffers are overly aggressive toward attendees. But, according to my own attendee surveys, that's the exception, not the rule. The single biggest complaint attendees have about exhibit staffers is that staffers ignore them. Unbelievable, but true.

Actually, the reason is simple. The most difficult moment at a trade show is for the staffer to simply talk to a stranger. Once they get the conversation going, they're OK. But walking up and starting a conversation is tough. We're out of our comfort zone. We're afraid of being rejected by somebody. And, of course, few of us have ever been trained to work in this uncomfortable environment.

Attendees are out of their comfort zone, too. They know they are the prey, and exhibit staffers are the hunters. Do you remember playing tag as a kid? When my friends and I played, we always had a safe zone called home. As long as we were touching that safe zone, the person who was "it" couldn't get us. Attendees at trade shows have their own safe zone, too. It's the aisle. Have you ever watched attendees walk down an empty aisle? They walk right down the middle, as far away from staffers as possible. And as long as they are walking in the aisle, they feel safe from the attacks of booth personnel, free to examine the exhibits without fear of being disturbed.

So we've got both the staffers and the attendees afraid of each other. What do we do?

As I wrote earlier, trade shows are uncomfortable for all of us. We are usually in a strange, noisy location, surrounded by people we don't know. It can be a little bit frightening. As booth personnel, we must do whatever we can to make an attendee feel comfortable with us. We must appear nonthreatening.

Attendees often walk with what I call the *trade show pace and gaze*. They stroll through the aisles with their eyes fixed on one of two levels. They're either looking for products displayed at waist-height levels, or signs about eight feet high. In other words, they aren't looking at you. In fact, they will do everything they can to avoid looking a salesperson in the eye. Therefore, an initial objective is to break the attendee out of his or her hypnotic step and stare. For the most part, the booth design and product presentation (if done effectively) will take care of breaking the pace. The exhibit's responsibility is to slow the attendee down; the salesperson then takes over and captures his or her attention.

The attendee is a person and wants to be treated as such. The first step in the trade show selling process is to put the attendee at ease. Therefore, the opening line should not be a selling line. It needs to be a comfortable icebreaker that shows the attendee you understand he or she is a human being.

The name badge may give you an easy opener, such as:

- "Hi, I see you're from Tucson. I went to school there. Is the Tack Room still open?"
- "How are you enjoying the show so far?"
- "Hi, I see you work for Consolidated Marketing. Do you know Marv and Sherwin?"
- "Whew, are your feet as tired as mine?"
- "I saw you look in our booth. Was there something here that caught your eye?"

Openers slow attendees down and get them talking. You want to be as natural as possible; don't sound mechanical. In other words, don't use the same opener with every person you meet or, after a while, you'll sound like a broken record. The following are four qualifications for effective opening lines.

1. It must break through preoccupation. An attendee has many other things on his or her mind. The attendee may be thinking the show is overwhelming, or that he or she shouldn't be away from the office. Remembering appointments and thinking about possible purchases are also distracting thoughts. Your opener needs to break through that preoccupation and get attention focused on you.

2. It must focus on the individual. Again, the idea is to make the attendee feel important. By making a positive comment about him or her or asking his or her opinion, you make the attendee feel good.
3. It must create a bond between you and the attendee. The attendee is being bombarded with thousands of "buy me" signals throughout the show. A nonthreatening conversation makes an attendee feel more comfortable with you, thus creating a mutual bond.
4. It must let both of you play a little. We're all on our guard at trade shows, especially the attendees, who are being perpetually accosted. An effective opener brings a brief respite to the sensory overload they're experiencing. Introduce a short joke about the show, the exhibits, the other attendees, or life in general.

Once in a great while, prospects appear who look hot from the very start. They walk into your exhibit as if they work there. They go directly to the product that interests them and look at it. They may even pick it up to examine it closely. They exude the air of real buyers who will place an order. And, of course, the booth personnel climb over each other to get to these prospects.

Someone showing that much interest does not need an opening line. The best approach is to respond with interest in the visitors and their needs by moving right to the qualifying step. Use an open-ended question, such as, "I see you're interested in our new front-pronged widget. Do you have a need for it in your work?" Obviously, it's easy to engage this type of attendees. Just remember, they are rare. Too many salespeople stand around an exhibit waiting for this type of visitor to arrive. Don't be like that!

Two caveats about the eager-beaver prospect. First, be sure to take control of the conversation as soon as possible. If you let the prospect dominate you, you may never get to the qualifying step. Briefly answer any questions the prospect asks, but immediately follow up with a qualifying question. Second, beware the competition! They may come spying for information and act like interested prospects. Make sure you move into the qualifying step quickly, before you give away any proprietary information.

Here are two recommendations that can dramatically change the results of your show:

1. You must understand your *rejection tolerance quotient* (RTQ). (Hey, when you're a published author/consultant/speaker, you're *supposed* to come up with stuff like this.)

Your RTQ is essentially based on the type of personality you have. Do you mind walking up and starting a conversation with a complete stranger? If it doesn't bother you at all, you are a 10, on a scale of 1 to 10. Most likely, you also have no problem with cold calling.

People who rate a 10 on my RTQ scale are those who will stand out in the aisles and actually direct traffic into their exhibit. Most attendees will simply push on past them, and it doesn't bother a 10.

I actually saw a 12 once at an American Welding Society show in Philadelphia. While walking through the show, I noticed a man lying down in the aisle. He wasn't hurt. In fact, his eyes were wide open, hands crossed over his chest, and twiddling his thumbs. Attendees were actually *stepping* over him and walking on, as if he didn't exist. Finally, someone stopped, bent over and asked, "Are you OK?" He jumped up and said, "Yeah, come on into my booth!" He's a 12.

A 1, on the other hand, is someone who might actually hide behind the exhibit. Obviously, these people would have a hard time at a trade show.

Most of us are in between somewhere. The point of understanding your RTQ, though, is to prepare yourself for approaching a stranger. A 10 can just automatically launch into a business discussion with a stranger. Farther down the scale, we need to be a little more personal. We need to break the ice before getting into a business conversation.

By understanding your RTQ, you can come up with one or two possible opening questions or comments that will begin the conversation. Remember, for most of us, we are at a trade show to look for new relationships. We *have* to talk with strangers. We don't have any choice.

2. Once you come up with your opening lines, you want to practice the SFTF Rule—the Speak First, Ten Foot Rule.

I first observed this in practice at a Ritz Carlton hotel several years ago. Every time I walked near a hotel employee, they made direct eye contact and then *said* something. It might be something as simple as "good morning," but they always said something. I learned later on that this was an established policy for employees. Whenever a guest came near, they had to make eye contact and say something.

I realized this was a great tool for exhibitors. So make it a corporate policy that whenever an attendee comes within 10 feet, staffers must, they must, they *must* say something.

I can safely say that of all the great tips and ideas you get from this book, the sftf Rule is, without question, the most valuable.

Qualify

After getting a prospect's attention, move quickly into the qualifying step of the selling process. Remember that time is a precious commodity, especially at a trade show. Don't think in terms of how many hours the show is open; think in terms of minutes. If a trade show is open a total of 26 hours, for example, look at it as 1,560 minutes. If you work at 100 percent efficiency and top speed, you'll see a new attendee every 6 minutes, or 260 people total for the show. But none of us are 100 percent efficient; none of us can go top speed all the time. Some hours are slower than others; you might only be 75 percent efficient. Some attendees will take more than 6 minutes of your time. There are many factors influencing how many people you talk to, but in order to be as efficient and effective as possible, you must control the situation. That's why it's so important not to waste time and to move to the qualifying step as soon as possible.

As I pointed out earlier, a good place to look for help is the name badge. Use it as you did in your introduction. If you know something about the company, it could be helpful in qualifying the attendee. Ask what area the attendee works in. What are his or her responsibilities? Once you find that out, you can determine how your product may help that company and whether the prospect has the authority to influence the buying decision. If you don't know anything about the company, find out.

Some shows color-code badges. At the 1995 Super Show, the giant exposition for the sporting goods industry, badges were color-coded as follows:

- Buyer—red
- Consultant—orange
- Exhibitor—blue
- Financial analyst—brown
- Manufacturer's representative—green
- Press/photographer—green
- Supplier to the industry—fuschia

What a great way to help prequalify attendees! (Of course, it doesn't help if you're color-blind.)

If you exhibit at a show with color-coded badges, be sure to include that information in your preshow meetings with your staff. Specifically target certain badge colors and let the others alone. For example, you might only be interested in talking to retailers, catalogers, and department store buyers. By instructing your staff to be on the lookout for turquoise, navy blue, and aqua badges, you effectively screen out many passersby. After all, you don't want to waste your time with unqualified prospects. If the show doesn't have color-coded badges, and most of them don't, it's up to you to carry the responsibility for qualifying the attendee.

Why qualify leads?   There are three reasons for qualifying leads at a trade show. The first is economics. Every contact you make with a prospect costs money. By qualifying at a show, you save money. The second is time. Every sales contact costs money as well as time. We all know that timing often has much to do with the success of making a sale. By delaying the qualifying process until after a show, the chance arises that a competitor might close a deal with a prospect first. By qualifying at a show, you keep one step ahead of the competition. The third reason is ease. My father used to tell me to follow the KISS principle—Keep It Simple, Salesman. He told me that eliminating any unnecessary steps in the process saves headaches and potential problems. Change KISS to QISS—Qualifying Is Smart Selling.

What if you can't qualify at a show?   Once in a great while a company can't qualify at a show. Usually, one of two factors causes this situation. The first is that the product is a runaway hit and appeals to nearly everybody at the show. The second reason is that the company has a small salesforce.

MicroDisk Services of Redmond, Washington, had such a situation in New York at PC Expo. With only two salespeople staffing the booth, it had a product that interested many attendees. The crowds were so large that it wasn't unusual for a salesperson to give a presentation to 50 people at once—an impossible situation for qualifying each contact. The solution came from Molin/Cutler Telemarketing Services of Seattle. MicroDisk turned over nearly 1,000 leads from the show and let Molin/Cutler's trained telemarketing reps qualify for them. By determining the strongest prospects, MicroDisk was then able to give those leads to its in-house people for solid follow-up. Within one month of the show, these efforts generated more than $1 million in signed business with 15 national accounts, plus another $1 million expected within the next 12 months.

Defining "qualified." The definition of qualified depends on your main objective. If it is to generate new leads and the only prospect you're looking for is a department store buyer, a navy blue badge may be all you need to qualify him. Then again, you may have a more horizontal market and are looking for anyone who uses PCs in the office. In that case, you are merely looking for purchase probability. Or, you may have a product with a short shelf life. In that case, you are looking for purchase probability within a specific time frame. Such diversity makes it imperative that you and your entire staff understand what qualified means.

There are four areas of criteria I look for in qualified prospects:

1. Are they decision makers, influencers, or specifiers? Which of these, or what combination, fit the target prospects I'm looking for?
2. What is their need and how does my product or service help to fill that need?
3. Do they have the ability to pay? Are they big enough to buy my product? Do they have money designated in their budget for this specific service?
4. When will they be in the market to buy my product or service? Thirty days? Six months? Two years?

It's critical to define qualified precisely. Looking for the presidents of Fortune 500 companies in the market for a $10 million computer system for installation in the next 18 months? Or for an account manager who wants a better software program for tracking receivables that he or she can install next week for less than $1,000? There's a big difference between those two prospects and a big difference in the potential number of attendees fitting those two descriptions.

Qualified to a "Tee"

Many years ago, before I joined the real world, I was a PGA golf professional. One of the most valuable lessons I learned as a player was to plan each hole backward before I played it.

Imagine, for example, you are playing golf on a par four hole. (*Par* basically refers to the length of a hole. A par four is long enough for it to require a minimum of two shots to reach the green and an average of two putts to get the ball into the hole.) Average golfers will play the hole in the fashion referred to as tee-to-green. In other words, they will plan to hit their first shot (the drive) as far as possible. After they have done that, they plan how to play the next shot to the green. The length and direction of the first shot determines what type of club they use in the second shot. They then hit the second shot toward the hole and, as before, the third shot depends on the length and direction of the second. When they finally reach the green, they plan their putts.

As a professional tournament player, however, I first play the hole backward in my mind. Using the same par four as an example, I determine where the hole is on the green and where I want to putt from. Greens are often rolling and slanted and there are certain spots from which it is easier to putt. After determining where I want my ball to be on the green, I go backward down the fairway and find the ideal location for my ball to be in order to hit it to that selected spot on the green. Again, there will be a location best suited for this shot. Once I've selected this location I know where I want to aim my first shot from the tee. It's not unusual for this method to completely change the type of club used at the tee and in the fairway.

Just like the golf professional who plays "green-to-tee," a trade show sales professional works backward in determining how to qualify a prospect. Ask yourself who the ideal customer is. What is that person like? What characteristics does that person possess? What position does he or she hold in the company? What size company does the prospect work for? How many people report to him or her? What size database does the prospect work with? How many stores does he or she own? Does he or she have a need to send documents overnight? How often does the prospect use the telephone? Where is the prospect located? How big is his or her budget?

Get out a pencil and write down a detailed description of your ideal customer. You can use a separate piece of paper, but if you fill in the blanks that follow, you'll always know where to look.

You may want to create such a description for every show you exhibit at. Because many shows are geared to a specific vertical market, your targets may vary from show to show.

My ideal customer:

1.

2.

3.

4.

5.

6.

Once you've described your ideal customer in detail, work backward to ask leading questions that will give you the information necessary to qualify potential customers. Be sure these are open-ended questions, asking: Who? What? Where? When? Why? How? How much? How many? Which? Following are some specific questions that may help you develop your criteria for prospects.

- Who is involved in the decision-making process?
- What are their specific responsibilities?
- Where is their company located? Is it within our geographical distribution area?
- When do they anticipate a need for this type of product?
- Why are they interested in our product?
- How do they plan to utilize this new product?
- How much money do they have in their budget?
- How many people will be using this product?
- Which area of the company will use it the most?

While you are qualifying an attendee, take the opportunity to detail how your product will help in several of these areas. Gear your responses to specific needs, focusing on specific problem areas the prospect may have. That's true selling.

These types of open-ended questions help you control the conversation. This is important. There are only two directions to go after the qualifying step. One is to determine that this visitor is not a qualified lead, at which point you politely end the conversation and move on to the next attendee. The second direction is to determine that this visitor is a qualified prospect. If this is the case and you present your product as a problem solver during the conversation, the prospect should see its value.

Remember the lead card example back in Chapter 3? This is the time to pull it out and put the information in writing. Do it as soon as you determine you are talking with a qualified prospect—waiting until after the conversation ends is a mistake. There are four good reasons to fill out a lead card while interviewing a prospect:

1. Memory is unreliable. How much can you forget within a few minutes? Plenty. Plus, with the circus-like distractions of a trade show, it's doubly hard to remember specific points of discussion. Write them down while you're talking with the prospect.
2. Time is valuable. Remember, you only have a finite number of minutes at a trade show. Even if it only takes a couple of minutes to scribble a few notes after a prospect leaves, you are wasting time. If you average 9.5 minutes on each prospect contact, that comes to 6.3 contacts per hour, or 176 contacts for a 28-hour show; if you add two more minutes to each contact to fill out the lead card, the time spent per contact comes to 11.5 minutes; that's only 5.2 contacts per hour, or 146 total show contacts. That's a 17 percent loss of contacts. It's not worth it. Write the information down while talking to a prospect.
3. It's professional. Prospects are impressed, not insulted when a salesperson takes notes. They feel it demonstrates a real interest in getting the right facts. And, as a matter of fact, you are.
4. It creates a sense of obligation in the prospect. Your goal in this conversation may be to set a follow-up appointment for after the show. Once you've begun to write down information on a lead card, you've created a sense of obligation with the prospect to at least be willing to go to that next step.

Uncover and Introduce

At the Uncover stage, remember that you are not giving a complete sales presentation; you are only presenting an overview of how your particular product can help a prospect based on one or two specific needs. You're not trying to make the sale; you're trying to accomplish your objective. This is one of the big differences between field selling and trade show selling. In the first, you may be used to more relaxed interactions, controlled in large part by the prospect. At the trade show, you must control the situation and keep it moving.

Exceptions to these rules arise, and you should keep your eye out for them. The prospect who is truly in a buying mode and could possibly be sold at the show deserves more time and attention. The big buying team that is comparison shopping at the show and potentially represents a sizable order is another example. Be alert for all opportunities and exceptions.

If you do run into one of these situations, use time away from the show to close the deal. Meet at your hotel or over dinner to iron out the details. This practice gives both of you the opportunity to utilize the show fully, and it provides you with an unhurried, distraction-free atmosphere.

Postshow Agreement

After a nonthreatening opening, a thorough job of presenting your product, and qualifying the prospect, the close naturally follows. If your objective is to get the prospect to agree to a follow-up sales call after the show, all you need to do is ask for an appointment. Or maybe your close is simply asking if you can telephone next Tuesday morning.

The point is, you must get new prospects to agree to that next step, whatever it is. Too often, we attempt to follow up with someone after a show, only to be greeted with, "Did I visit your booth? I don't remember." You want to tag their memory with a specific, postshow step. That way, you can say something like, "I'll send you this information immediately after the show. Would it be OK if I followed up with you next Friday to make sure you received the information?"

Basically, all you're doing in the close is restating the prospect's needs and reiterating how your products will help satisfy those needs. Then you follow with a statement like, "Then you would agree that we should meet again in two weeks to discuss this further?" Even though it's short and simple, this step is important. By closing, you establish future contact with the prospect. If you go through the other steps without the close, you risk losing a potential sale. In a sense, the trade show close is much like closing in the field, with one notable difference: At the show, you close on an agreement to move to the next step in the sales relationship process, not the product.

Team Signals

Every once in a while, you will run into a circumstance outside of show selling that still requires teamwork. There are two common situations:

The "Leech."   This is actually a not-so-nice term for unqualified attendees who won't let you go. Politely tell them you've enjoyed the conversation, but you know they want to see other exhibits and you need to get back to work. It usually works. In a situation where they don't take the hint, use a team signal. A prearranged signal—a tug on the ear, a finger across the nose (à la The Sting), whatever—can indicate your predicament to your booth mates. Once they pick it up, they can approach you with a reminder of a fictitious appointment or some other devious device. The point is to get you away as quickly as possible.

The "Complainer."   Occasionally, somebody has a problem with your accounts receivable department and decides to take it up personally with the president of your company. Often the intention is to simply make a scene at a crowded show with the notion that it will hurt your business. Without going into a complete discussion of what planet we should blast these nasties off to, it's important to plan for them. If such a situation arises, the first thing to do is get these people out of your exhibit as quickly as possible. One way of doing this is to appoint a daily ombudsman responsible for handling unhappy people. Have the appointed troubleshooter take them out for a cup of coffee over which to discuss their problems.

Subliminal Signals

A trade show may be as small as a few dozen exhibits or as large as several thousand. In either case, attendees walking through the aisles are no more comfortable being surrounded by strangers than you are. Because of this, it's important to be aware of the fine art of nonverbal communication.

Attendees walking through the exhibit area move at the *trade show pace.* At the same time, they develop the *trade show gaze,* mentally culling out exhibits, effectively eliminating different booths from consideration. They may do this without even stopping to talk with us. Or they may do it within 15 seconds of meeting us! In effect, they are looking for reasons to cross us off their list.

I learned something interesting from my good friend George Walther, one of the country's leading telemarketing experts. In his seminars, George often pairs people up with a total stranger, turns out the lights, and has the two people talk to each other. George has the two discuss a very ordinary topic—their favorite dessert, the last vacation they had, their respective hobbies. George only lets the first person talk for about 13 seconds, then switches for another 13 seconds.

After this exercise, George shows the audience a list of adjectives. Included in the list are such words as shy, confident, assertive, sharing, thoughtful, caring, honest, intelligent, and friendly. The two people then select three or four words from the list that would describe their partner. People are amazed at how accurately others can read them in less than a quarter of a minute, after only hearing their voices.

Obviously, George is showing people how our telephone voices sound, but the same type of "instant analyzation" is going on when we meet people at a trade show. And because of the nature of trade shows, a brief encounter is usually all we get with an attendee. In the 1996 Exhibit Surveys, Inc. report on Best Remembered Exhibits, the smaller your exhibit, the more important your staff becomes. Size of booth and interest in products were the only factors more important. Because that encounter is so brief, nonverbal communicative skills are probably more important at trade shows than in any other selling situation.

Reading Your Prospect

Before we consider how to improve our body language, let's learn to read the body language of attendees. As visitors walk by your booth, watch for those subliminal signals that will open the door for the first approach. Watch how they walk, stand, and use their hands. Look at their eyes. Do they look like they want to talk? Remember the trade show pace and gaze? Attendees get into this steady pace at a show to protect themselves. But once something has caught their eyes, it breaks the pace. Keep your own eye open for this break. If it's in front of your booth, it's probably something you're displaying that slows them down. Once you see that, it's time to engage.

Notice how they stand. Do their shoulders still aim down the aisle or have they squared them into your display? The more their body shows an inclination toward your exhibit, the more interested they are.

Watch for hand and arm signals from the prospect:

Palm rubbing.   This is a positive sign, usually of eagerness, anticipation, or anxiousness. Follow the signal and move ahead.

Touching the face.   This action means a person is thinking about what you've just said, maybe about how your product will fit into an office system. The best action here is to be quiet and wait for the prospect to take the next lead.

Steepling.   Have you ever been with people who put their elbows on a chair's armrest and steeple their hands? This is one of the most powerful subliminal gestures people can make. It represents power, knowledge, and confidence. Prospects who use this signal know what they want, and, apparently, you're giving the right information. If they are steepling and touching their face, it's a good sign of interest. Be careful not to use this signal yourself too early in the conversation—you might come across as cocky.

Arms folded.   This action is a classic protective gesture. People who use this are saying, "Don't bother me." Perhaps you haven't made your visitor feel comfortable. Slow down your presentation and work on assuring your customer before you proceed any further. Be more casual and empathetic toward the attendee. Once the arms are relaxed, move on with the process.

Clenched fists.   I don't have to tell you this is a bad signal. Use the same tactics to regain your client's interest that you would with crossed arms.

Legs crossed at ankles.   This may be a defensive gesture, much like crossed arms—handle it the same way. Be careful, though; the prospect may just be tired from a long day. According to Exhibit Surveys, Inc., in 1997 the average attendee spent 8.4 hours on the show floor. That's a lot of wear on the feet. So, if ankles are crossed, watch to see if the prospect also shifts weight from foot to foot; if so, it's indicative of weariness, in which case you've got to work a little harder to hold the prospect's attention.

Sudden gestures. Don't automatically assume that any of the above gestures are good or bad. Are their arms crossed? Maybe they're cold, not defensive. (Maybe you're cold, too.) The thing to watch for is an abrupt change in body language. If they seemed open and comfortable with you and then suddenly folded their arms, it might have been something you just said or showed. Stop the presentation and say something like, "I see you're concerned. Did I say something that bothers you?," or, "You seem bothered about our terms. Would you share your concerns with me?"

Become a student of prospects and be aware of any changes in their subliminal signals. If you miss one of these signals and continue your presentation, you could lose a prospect.

Proxemics

Proxemics is the study of personal space. The important thing to understand in regard to proxemics is the comfort zone and how it relates to the selling process. There are three distinct zones extending outward from each individual. (See Figure 6-1.)

Figure 6-1 Our Personal Space

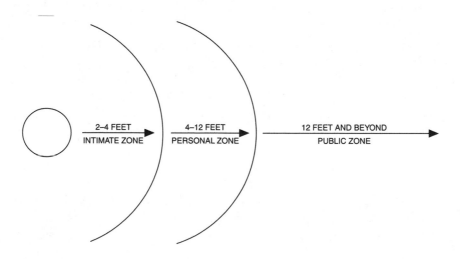

The outermost zone, known as the *public zone,* begins approximately 12 feet away from us and extends outward. Anybody in this zone is not deemed to be someone to pay attention to. In other words, it's not important for us to acknowledge anyone who is 12 feet or farther away. In a trade show, you wouldn't be able to sell people your product if they were farther than 12 feet away. Conversely, attendees know that they are safe as long as they keep their distance.

The middle zone, known as the *personal zone,* extends from approximately four to 12 feet away. Anybody entering this zone can now be attended to. At a trade show, this zone is where the selling process begins. When an attendee allows you to enter this zone, you are given unspoken permission to begin communicating. Opening and qualifying steps take place in this zone.

The closest zone, known as the *intimate zone,* extends up to two to four feet away from the body. This is where selling occurs. If someone allows you to enter this zone while you're talking about your product, you will have a much easier time of selling.

Since an arm's length is approximately three feet, the phrase "an arm's length transaction" could be translated into, "Don't let the salesperson get near your intimate zone!" Respect the attendees' personal space. Don't move in too close too quickly. Wait until you receive signals giving you permission. If prospects touch you on the arm while in conversation, it's a positive sign. Likewise, if they lean toward you while listening to your presentation, they're giving you permission to lean in too.

One last word about proxemics. Just as animals in the jungle stake out territory, so will humans. Be careful you don't do that in your exhibit. Don't leave any of your personal things—briefcase, notepad, date book—around for people to see. They send a territorial signal. Keep such things out of sight. The exhibit is meant to be warm and inviting to the attendee, not threatening.

Subliminal Selling at the Booth

Trade shows exemplify the truth of the phrase, "You never get a second chance to make a good first impression." The communication process begins before attendees even step into our exhibit. By consciously sending warm, confident, positive signals at all times, you tell attendees that you are someone worth knowing. Let's look at how subliminal signals affect our performance and how we can use them to our advantage.

The stance.   When standing in the booth waiting for a prospect (yes, I said *standing*—never sit!), your stance alone tells the prospect a lot. Stand with your feet about shoulder width apart, weight evenly balanced, and your hands either hanging at your side or clasped behind your back. Such a stance is open and powerful.

Don't shift your weight from foot to foot or cross your legs at the ankles. These are weak positions, indicative of defensiveness to an attendee. It's hard to keep from doing this when your feet are tired at the end of a long show day, but that visitor at 4:00 P.M. may be your biggest catch of the day. Remain alert! One way to control this distracting behavior is to wear comfortable shoes during the show.

If you have anything to say about booth design and construction, buy a good pad to go under your carpet. Not only will you feel a big difference in your own legs and feet, but so will the attendees. They'll spend more time in your exhibit, and they won't know why. Another subliminal selling technique.

The handshake.   Ah, the almighty handshake! I have actually had buyers tell me they didn't order from a particular salesperson because of his or her handshake. Its importance cannot be overstated.

The handshake is how you and the prospect measure each other's strength and purpose. If you have a weak, sweaty, fragile, trembling grip, prospects immediately assume you are a pushover; they'll feel confident that they can turn you down and send you on your way. If your grip is weak, build it up. Get a grip strengthener at a sporting goods store, or just squeeze a tennis ball. To combat sweaty palms, wash your hands frequently, don't clasp them together while standing around, and leave them out of your pockets; let the air dry them out. Carry moist towelettes so you won't have to constantly leave the booth to wash your hands. Also, don't let an attendee see you wiping them on your clothes—an instant loss of points.

Offer your hand first to your visitors, but wait for them to let go first. Never end a handshake too early. Don't use the two-handed shake unless you know the person well. People tend to be suspicious of someone using that type of "politician's" handshake at the first meeting. Shake hands firmly, but not bone-crushingly. Some people want to show off how strong they are. It's unnecessary and annoying.

> **Men:** When you first meet attendees, a useful trick to use in gaining control quickly is to pull the prospects toward you a little

as you shake. It shows warmth and lack of fear. Don't worry if they pull back slightly. You've established who's in control of the upcoming conversation. I do not recommend women try this. Unfortunately, if a man is on the receiving end, he may interpret it as an advance. A woman receiving such a handshake from another woman may be put off.

Women: If your hand is small and you're shaking hands with a large person, spread your fingers a slight bit, giving the impression of a larger grip. This helps to keep you from being perceived as small and frail.

Hands and arms.   While waiting for an attendee, stand with your hands at your side or clasped behind your back. Never cross your arms or put your hands in your pockets. These positions send out a defensive or rude signal. While engaging a prospect, use open-palmed gestures with your elbows away from your body. This denotes a warm, welcoming posture.

When listening, keep your hands unclenched and visible. This sends a nonverbal message of, "I trust you and you can trust me." Don't take the chance of scaring off a visitor. The first minute is crucial to the success of the encounter. Once you've made an attendee feel comfortable and confident through your opening and qualifying steps, you'll be in a better position to move quickly into the close.

Eye contact.   Salespeople at a trade show must make a special effort to maintain eye contact with the person to whom they are talking. There are so many other interesting things to look at and so many faces going by that the temptation to look everywhere except in your prospect's eyes is very strong. Many of us have been told to maintain pseudo eye contact by looking at a point on the tip of a person's nose or at the middle of the forehead. This process of depersonification is frequently counterproductive. People know when someone is avoiding eye contact.

When you look in people's eyes, you tend to check one eye, then the other. When you stare at a nose, your eyes are locked onto one point; prospects will sense something is wrong. If you are standing face-to-face and closer than five feet apart at a show, prospects with normal vision will be able to see that you aren't looking into their eyes. So, avoid tricks that can only hurt your chances by offending a potential lead. Look directly into your prospects' eyes and maintain that connection.

Building Rapport

People like to communicate with people who are like them. Talk to them in their style and show you care for them as individuals. Reaching this harmonious connection in a brief few minutes can be done; it brings trust, which in turn gains sales. If you use rapport skills, opportunities will come to you.

Rapport is the bridge that helps the person you're communicating with find meaning and intent in the things you say. It helps them feel comfortable with you and creates a feeling of warmth and understanding. Most importantly, when it comes to selling, rapport helps your prospects feel that what you're saying is directed right at them, aimed at their particular needs and desires. Without rapport, you're just communicating information. You might as well just read your presentation to the prospects. The best way to generate rapport is to empathize genuinely and sincerely with your prospects' needs or desires. No technique will work unless you really care about the people you're dealing with.

I can't show you how to care, but I can explain some verbal and non-verbal techniques that develop rapport quickly:

Mirroring.   People tend to do business with or put the most trust in people who are like them. If you are radically different from the attendee, it will take longer to build the warmth and trust necessary to make a sale. One of the ways you can quickly build trust and rapport is to mirror body movement and posture.

If you observe people who enjoy being around each other, you'll notice an unconsciously high amount of physical rapport. Adversaries, on the other hand, will often deliberately, though unconsciously, mismatch movements. They'll even go so far as to break eye contact to prevent rapport from accidentally being created.

During any interaction with attendees, watch their body movements closely. If they cross their arms, cross yours. If they put their arms by their side, put your arms by your side. When they lean forward, lean forward, too. If you do this subtly, your prospects will have no idea of what you are doing, and you'll be amazed at how quickly high rapport between you occurs. Mirroring body movements is really a by-product of having incredibly high rapport.

Matching.   Use key words and phrases that hold significance for your customer. People have a style of talking and a particular lexicon that is meaningful to them. If you can identify their style and key phrases, you'll have the key to unlock their mind.

Different industries have their own style of talking. Attorneys have "legalese" and stock brokers have "brokerese." The particular industry your prospect belongs to will have a vocabulary peculiar to itself; be sure to learn its key words and phrases so you can communicate more effectively. A good example of jargon is the word *networking*. This is an overused term in entrepreneurial circles these days, but a different version of the term is used in other industries. In the real estate market, the word *farming* means the same thing. And in some questionable industries, the word *pyramiding* has been used interchangeably with networking.

Verbal rapport.   The best way to establish verbal rapport with attendees is to listen intently for the first minute or so, making a mental note of what you hear. Listen for inflection patterns, length of sentences, and certain key words or phrases. You can communicate with them subliminally by subtly duplicating their speaking patterns. As long as you're not mimicking them in a sarcastic manner, they'll hardly notice. People expect you to talk the way they do. When you don't communicate in a style that is comfortable to the prospects, you cause tension.

Anchoring.   This is more or less a reverse style of matching for building rapport. When anchoring a prospect, you are using a key word, phrase, or physical movement of your own to anchor specific good feelings and emotions. For example, when I speak before a group, I'll often begin by telling a humorous story about my past experience as a professional golfer. Usually the story is about something that, at the time, was embarrassing, but is now funny. As I hit the punch line, I make a certain face, usually a look of naive bewilderment to match the look on my face at the time of the incident. Usually, the combination of how I tell the story and my expression will draw laughter from the audience.

The interesting thing that then happens is that during my subsequent speech or seminar, I can make that same face to draw laughter. I've learned to use that face to elicit good feelings at specific times during the course of the program. The people in the audience have been subconsciously programmed through my initial story to believe that when I make that face, they are supposed to feel good. I've anchored that good feeling.

The same effect can be achieved with a certain word or phrase. Comedian Joan Rivers uses, "Can we talk?" For Ronald Reagan, it's "There you go again." Rodney Dangerfield says, "I get no respect."

In a selling situation, if it's possible to anchor a word or physical movement to a good feeling with the prospect, it's possible to elicit that same feeling when closing the sale.

A salesperson used this technique on me at a local Nordstrom department store. I was looking for a new suit, and I decided to stop in and try some on. The salesperson who walked up to help came straight out and said, "You're very handsome!" While I was basking in the compliment and thanking her, she touched me lightly on the elbow. First, she took the chance of invading my intimate zone; I didn't mind, however, because of the compliment. Second, she anchored my good feelings by touching my elbow.

I wasn't having any success with the $200 to $300 suits, when she suggested I try on a $600 suit. I reluctantly agreed to do it, knowing full well I was wasting her time and mine. I'd never spend that kind of money on a suit! As I came out of the dressing area, she walked right up and commented, "That suit looks great on you!" And, you guessed it, she touched me on the elbow exactly like she had earlier. The suit did look great on me, but her touching my elbow helped elicit the same good feelings I felt when she said I was handsome. I bought the suit.

Caution About Subliminal Signals

These little tricks are not for everybody. If you feel uncomfortable using them, then don't. Your first and foremost objective is to help the customer, not con him. These subliminal techniques are powerful in helping you develop an early rapport with a prospect, but if you don't have a strong desire to help your customer solve problems, these tools will only be misused.

CHAPTER 7

Secrets of Successful Shows

Trade Show Basics

This section could be called "Trade Show 101." I often get criticized during presentations to salespeople that all this is common knowledge. My response is, "Then why don't you act on it?" I know for a fact that two hours into the first day of a trade show, I can stand in an aisle and watch the vast majority of staffers breaking each of these simple rules. They might be common sense, but they certainly aren't common practice.

Don't Sit

If you sit during a trade show, you give attendees the impression that you don't care to be bothered. Attendees will not interrupt your private time, if they perceive it as such. Remember, too, attendees are also looking for reasons to disqualify you. Don't give them any. In addition, as the saying goes, if you act enthusiastic, you'll be enthusiastic. The reverse is also true. If you act bored, you'll be bored . . . and boring.

Don't Read

For every 10 feet of linear space, you have just two to three seconds to impress attendees enough to get them to stop. It's not impressive to see someone reading a newspaper or magazine. Save it for later.

Don't Smoke

Not only is it impolite—and perhaps even illegal—to smoke in your booth, but it can actually offend a prospective customer. It's OK, however, to keep ashtrays in the booth for attendees' use. If you really need that cigarette, schedule breaks to go somewhere else to smoke.

Don't Eat or Drink at the Exhibit

It's just plain rude and messy. Potential customers won't bother you while you're eating; they're too polite. And, of course, there are lots of other exhibits where people are waiting to sell. They don't need to talk to you.

Don't Chew Gum

No one wants to talk with someone who's chomping away on a piece of gum. Plus, trade shows are noisy. You need to be able to speak clearly and, sometimes, loudly. You can't communicate well with something in your mouth. For the same reason, avoid breath mints. It's a good idea to have some breath spray or drops handy, but avoid anything that takes up space in your mouth for any length of time.

Don't Ignore Prospects

One of the rudest things you can do is ignore a prospect, even for a few seconds. Nobody likes to be ignored. If you're busy when someone approaches, either acknowledge the person or try to include him or her in your conversation. If you're talking to a booth mate or neighbor, break it off immediately.

Don't Talk on the Telephone

Why do you need a phone in your booth anyway? Every minute you spend on the phone is one less minute you could be talking to prospects, and like other trade show prohibitions, it's rude. Even if the show is slow, it only takes one good prospect to make it successful. If you're on the phone, you may miss that person.

Don't Be a Border Guard

Although you want to stand close to the aisle to acknowledge attendees walking by, don't stand where you become a barricade or block the view. Stand near the aisle and off to the side, especially if you're in a 10-foot booth. (See Figure 7-1.)

Don't Hand Out Literature to Everyone

I already talked about this a little in a previous chapter, but let's discuss it in greater detail.

If you've ever walked through Manhattan, you've probably had the honor of being accosted by some odd-looking person holding a pile of flyers, who, as you approach, thrusts one practically into your face. Even if the literature is potentially interesting, this bold approach is offensive. So, you walk quickly away, looking for the nearest trash can. Some people don't even wait to find one—they just drop the handout on the ground. When you think about it, it's not so different from those people at trade shows who stand in the aisle in front of their booths and thrust literature at unsuspecting attendees. Do you really want prospective customers to see you in that light?

Figure 7-1 Where to Stand in Your Booth

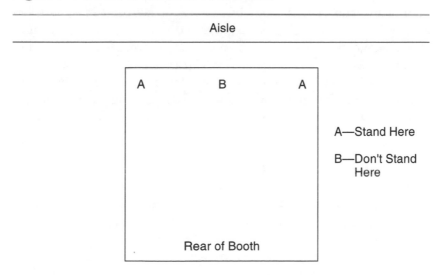

Furthermore it's expensive. Here's a money-saving tip: Take only one-fourth as many pieces of literature as you originally planned. Give them all out on the first day of the show. At the end of the day, walk to the nearest trash can, empty it out, and collect your literature. Voila! Now you've got the next day's inventory for distributing. At the end of each day, you can repeat this procedure.

Sarcasm aside, it's just not necessary to give literature to people at the show, even if they ask for it. Some specific reasons follow:

Expense.   The cost of printing brochures and flyers is astronomical. Look at each brochure as cash—do you really want to pass out money to anybody who asks for it? Of course not. When you arbitrarily give away your literature, you can bet most of it will end up in the circular file. The cost of shipping literature, too, is staggering. Shippers charge you by weight, and paper is heavy. There are better ways to spend your money.

No attendee interest.   You don't want your expensive literature lost in the crowd. If the show is large, attendees may collect hundreds of pieces of literature. To avoid taking it back on the airplane, they'll cull through it at the hotel, spending about 1.3 seconds on each brochure, selecting the ones that interest them the most (about 7 flyers) and tossing the other 153 four-color catalogs in the trash. Even if the show is small, it's still not practical to give out literature. No buyer wants to lug around pounds of superfluous paper.

Mailing literature later is good business.   So how do you get valuable information to hot prospects? Mail it. Tell prospects that you don't want to weigh them down with more literature, that you will send the requested information after the show. By doing so, you accomplish several objectives.

First, you show your professionalism. By saying you're going to do something and then doing it, you show you are dependable. And, as Humphrey Bogart might remark, "That's the beginning of a beautiful relationship." Second, you can personalize the follow-up with a letter. Mention some specific needs the prospect brought out in your discussion; talk about something personal you remember from the show. Was the prospect wearing something distinctive? Did he or she mention playing golf? Referring to such things establishes a positive rapport. Finally, it gives you a good reason to follow up by telephone. This technique creates a sense of obligation on the prospect's part to take your call. It's much easier to confirm that the prospect received the requested material than to call out of the blue and say you met at the show. Calling then gives you an open door for moving forward in the selling process.

If you arbitrarily give out literature, you're taking a big chance. If you call, prospects may or may not remember you, and may or may not still have your literature.

Don't Talk with Other Booth Personnel

I can't repeat this enough. If you give attendees a reason not to stop by your exhibit, they won't. If you look like you're busy having a conversation with someone else, they won't bother you. Keep your conversation with your booth mates and neighboring exhibit staff to the bare minimum. Talk to your potential prospects, not buddies.

Don't Misjudge Appearance

I call this the *Edith Goldman Syndrome.* I believe Edith started the trend of women wearing athletic shoes for the walk to work. Edith has been doing this for years at trade shows. One day, after attending a few hundred trade shows around the world as a buyer, she finally got fed up with aching, tired feet. So she began to wear athletic shoes. Edith didn't care what she looked like. She just wanted to be comfortable, but not all exhibitors accepted Edith's style. She didn't look like a buyer. But she is—a big buyer, one of the head buyers for Leavitt Advertising/Hanover House Industries, one of the largest mail order catalog houses in the world. It publishes more than 20 different catalogs, including Adam York, Synchronics, and Tapestry. She was also instrumental in the start-up of one of TV's shopping channels.

Edith has the authority to buy for any part of Leavitt, which gives her considerable buying influence. But, because she wears running shoes to trade shows, not everyone takes her seriously. Edith is philosophical about it: "If they don't take me seriously, that's their loss, not mine." And she's right.

The only people who have to look good at the trade show are the exhibit staffers. Buyers can be as comfortable as they want—blue jeans, sports shirts, slacks, whatever. Don't underestimate them.

Don't Cluster

The subliminal aspects of trade shows cannot be overemphasized. If you get into a group discussion with two or more booth mates or other nonprospects, you're clustering. In the eyes of attendees, you look like a street-corner gang. They will steer clear of you because it's intimidating to approach a group of strangers. Create a warm, open, inviting atmosphere in your exhibit.

Be Enthusiastic

Platitudes about enthusiasm are widespread, but there's a reason for that. Enthusiasm works, and it's contagious. It's not necessary to jump up and down to be enthusiastic; in fact, enthusiasm can be defined as an activity in which a lively and absorbing interest is shown. Be enthusiastic about the show and its potential. Don't let others bring you down with negative attitudes. A truly successful person doesn't look at any project without enthusiasm.

Be enthusiastic about your company and its products. To the attendee, you are your company; however you look, act, and talk will have a major influence on how the attendee perceives your company. Besides, if you're not enthusiastic about your company and its products, how can you possibly expect anybody else to be?

Working with major corporations and top conventions, I often meet and work with well-known celebrities. A few years ago, I worked a show in Las Vegas with Hulk Hogan. (I guess that since he's left the World Wrestling Federation for the World Championship Wrestling, he's become "Hollywood Hulk" Hogan, but we all know him as Hulk.) Now, Hulk (we're on a first-name basis) is one of the most recognizable faces in the world and a darn smart marketer, too.

As it turned out, we flew out of Las Vegas together, on to another convention in Orlando. We were assigned seats next to each other. He had the aisle seat, and I had the window seat. Just before taking off, Hulk turned to me and said, "I'm going to take a nap. If you want to get up, just punch me." Hmmmm, I don't think so.

After the Hulkster woke up, we talked about the convention. He knew what I did, so I asked what his thoughts were about the exhibitors. Rolling his eyes, he said, "Hey, tell those guys to at least *act* like they want to be there! I walk aisles of trade shows, and I can tell that most exhibitors don't want to be there. They sit or stand in the back of their booth, hands in their pockets, scowls on their faces, sending clear signals to every attendee walking by. Tell them that even if they don't want to be there, at least *act* like they do!"

Hulk went on to explain that when he leaves his home in Texas to go to work, he puts on his "game face." In other words, his fans expect the Hulk to look and act a specific way, and he's not going to disappoint them, even if he's not really in the mood. He was simply pointing out that exhibitors need to put on their "game face," too. No matter how they feel.

I thought that was good advice. Enthusiasm is as critical to your company's success as anything.

Attire and Appearance

This might be a little out of your comfort zone, but it's important to discuss, nonetheless. Let's first talk about attire.

There seems to be a school of thought that if you're not dressed in a suit and tie, you're out of uniform and attendees won't take you seriously. Quite frankly, I come from the "get out loud" school of thought.

Many trade shows have hundreds, some over a thousand, exhibiting companies. The average attendee will spend only 8.4 hours on the trade show floor, having meaningful encounters with roughly 30 exhibitors. It is critical that you pull out all the stops to separate yourself from the crowd and be easily seen by attendees. If you and your staffers are dressed in suits and ties, you will look like everybody else in the expo hall.

There are three good reasons for not dressing in suits and ties:

1. You avoid blending in with the crowd. We need to utilize every opportunity available to us to draw attention to our booth and our company. Your preshow promotion does that. Your trade ads do that. Your exhibit design does that. Maybe even your products do that. Why not have your exhibit staffers do that?
2. You make it easier for the attendee to find a staffer. It's unbelievable to me how often I'll walk into an exhibit (especially a big one) and be totally unable to identify who works there. Exhibits are often packed with attendees wearing suits and ties, which makes it ridiculously difficult to find the staffers.
3. The staffers can't hide. This is a big deal. Many times staffers will complain about having to wear matching golf shirts. They holler, "It's not professional!" when what they're actually saying is, "Hey, I don't want to work this show. If I look like everybody else, I can hide a lot. But if I wear some type of identifiable uniform, people will be able to find me."

No kidding. Isn't that the idea? And this also prevents people from getting into those "street gangs" we've all seen in booths. Street gangs are those groups of staffers who congregate to talk about everything but business and totally ignore attendees. When they all have matching shirts or some other identifiable feature, they stick out like sore thumbs.

I'm not necessarily saying that you should look at golf shirts or sweaters, or blazers, or pith helmets. My basic rule of thumb is: look at what everybody else is doing and don't do that.

If I'm working with a company exhibiting at a show where we know most people will be wearing suits and ties, I go to the opposite end of the spectrum and will encourage staffers to be extremely casual. If, on the other hand, I'm working with an exhibitor at Surf Expo, where shorts and swim suits are the norm, I wear a suit.

Use the Prospect's Name

People love to hear their own names. Make attendees feel important by making a concerted effort to remember their name and use it in the conversation from time to time.

At trade shows, people always try to glance slyly at another person's name tag. What's all the secrecy about? You probably don't know attendees' names, so you aren't insulting them by looking at their badges. Be bold; look directly at the badge and repeat the name out loud. If you have trouble pronouncing a name, ask. Tell the attendee you want to be sure and get his or her name right because you know how important your own name is to you. Most attendees will be happy to teach you the proper pronunciation. And if it's a particularly unusual name, it might prove a great opener for you.

Know Your Competition

If there's one place you should be ready to stand up to your competition, it's at a trade show. When you talk about how your product compares with the ABC Corporation, you can bet the attendee is going to go over to the ABC booth and verify your statements.

Get as much information as you can about the competition before the show and make sure your sales staff knows all about them. Then, in addition to that information, assign one or two of your competitors exhibiting at that show to each of your sales staff. Have them go through your competitors' exhibits and get the lowdown on what's new. Try to get any information that will be helpful to your cause—pricing, product comparisons, terms, delivery, freight, and the like. Obviously, no competitor parts willingly with all that information, and if your salespeople stroll into their exhibit with your company's badges on display . . . well, you know what will happen. The way to get around this is to get everybody a second badge. Preregister them as retailers, dealers, distributors, anything that will get your competition to open up. Send them off to gather all the information possible on the first day, and debrief each other at that night's meeting.

Another way to get this information is through your customers. They'll give out a lot of helpful information. They'll even tell you what the positives and negatives are about the competition, and how you stack up.

Do I feel that telling you these schemes lacks integrity? Not really. I make this suggestion to every client and audience I have. Besides, while you're reading this little tip so is your competition. Don't say I didn't warn you.

Keep Moving in Your Booth

This is more for your own well-being than it is a selling tip, but it will make a difference if your booth is an island. By walking from one end of the booth to the other from time to time, you'll stimulate the blood flow in your legs and feet. Of course, I'm not talking about pacing back and forth; just plan to walk across the booth every few minutes or so. Standing for several hours creates a lot of strain on your lower body. Your legs can cramp up, and your feet will be aching for days. By exercising them periodically, you'll do yourself a big favor.

When you take a break, don't just go somewhere and sit down. Give your legs a chance to limber up. Go outside, walk around, and get some fresh air. You'll be surprised at the difference in how you'll feel at the end of the four days.

For those of you working island booths and peninsulas, you absolutely must keep moving. Your exhibit can act as a barricade to attendees. If you're on one side and attendees approach from the other, you might never see them if you aren't mobile. Stay out toward the perimeter and keep moving. Don't stay in one place too long—you might miss prospects completely.

Be Prompt and Be Prepared

Ideally, no one should work more than four hours a day at a trade show, but for some of us it's just not possible to have more than one shift. Many companies can only afford to send one or two people to a show, and they must be in the booth at all times. In these cases, being on time means being prepared when the show opens.

Even on a small budget, you can still project an image of professionalism to prospects and customers. Too often I've seen companies not ready to exhibit when the doors open. This happens not only on the first day, but every other day, too. For some reason, people seem to think that it doesn't matter if attendees see them still unpacking products stored overnight. It does. Every action you make in front of a prospective customer sends a message. Do you really want to project an image of someone who's unorganized and unkempt? What type of message do you suppose attendees receive when they see such things?

If your exhibit is all ready to go, get to the show at least 15 minutes before it opens. Put away your briefcase and coat and make sure the booth is clean. If you've stored product overnight, be there at least 30 minutes early to set up. Use any extra time to prepare yourself mentally for the coming day. If you're working all day on your feet, you'll need to program yourself mentally to have a good, positive attitude for the next eight hours.

If your company can afford to bring enough people to work shifts, make sure the staff shows up at least 15 minutes before their shift begins. A good idea is to overlap the shifts. If, for example, a show has hours of 10:00 A.M. to 6:00 P.M., you can run shifts like this:

9:30 A.M.–12:00 P.M.	Silver team
11:45 A.M.–2:00 P.M.	Gold team
1:45 P.M.–4:00 P.M.	Silver team
3:45 P.M.–6:30 P.M.	Gold team

This type of schedule allows enough time in the morning to set up before the doors open, a 15-minute overlap for shift change, and some extra time at the end of the day to store supplies for overnight and clean up. Although it may be a little crowded during changeover, it's a lot better to have too many salespeople than to have too few.

Be firm about the schedule. Demand that your people be on time, and don't tolerate laggards. A trade show is no place for someone who isn't going to support your system. I've known sales managers who actually sent salespeople home early rather than allow them to become a bad influence on the rest of the staff.

Get a Good Night's Sleep

It's common for salespeople to get together at night when they're out of town to have a little fun. There's no harm in that, but late hours are detrimental to a trade show. A trade show is hard, hard work. It's extremely tough on the body—the feet, the legs, the lower back, the eyes, and the voice. You need to give your body a chance to recuperate before the next day's onslaught. Don't go out partying until the wee hours; you'll pay for it the next day. You can't risk losing a new customer because you aren't sharp enough.

Make a concerted effort to plan rest time into your trade show calendar. Give yourself time to go back to your room and unwind before going to bed. Take a Jacuzzi or short walk to loosen up. Bring a good bedtime book to read, and I don't mean a business book. Give the right side of your brain a chance to calm down from the overload it went through during the day. And then get a good night's sleep. You'll feel a lot better the next day.

There's a bit of an ego bonus, too. When you arrive at the show fresh, you'll be able to needle all the other salespeople who show up with hangovers. Come to think of it, you'll probably be able to outsell them, too. What an interesting idea . . .

Refrain from Alcohol During
Trade Show Week

Alcohol is a depressant that slows down the physical and mental processes. Alcohol causes your brain to go into slow motion. Your lips stop working, even though your mouth might not. You might accidentally slip and let out confidential information. You might embarrass yourself in front of a customer or your boss. You could wake the next morning with a hangover and be a total waste at the show. Worse still, you might not be able to work the show. It's already been established that trade shows are hard work; don't do anything that will limit your potential for success.

If you're out with a customer or prospect, drink soft drinks or, better still, lots of water. Trade shows dehydrate the body, so drinking water replenishes natural fluids. And the kicker is that, like getting a good night's sleep, you'll feel better when you don't drink. You'll also have an edge on those salespeople who spent the night out swapping war stories at a bar.

Avoid Strange or Exotic Foods

When you travel out of town to a trade show, you don't have any choice but to eat out. Do your body a favor and stick to boring, nongreasy foods. You're only asking for trouble when you try something new and different at an exotic new restaurant or local favorite. If you're not used to eating dim sum, Cajun meat loaf, or Buffalo wings, then don't try them. Your body has a hard enough time when traveling, without stuffing it with a lot of foreign substances.

Appoint a Media Liaison

There's always a chance that the media might come by your booth for a story. They may be following up a lead your own company sent to them, or they may have heard about some new development or unusual products your company has introduced at the show. They may even have just strolled by and randomly selected your exhibit as one to cover for the 11:00 News. In any case, make sure you have one person assigned as the media's liaison with your company. That way you guarantee that the same story is being told at all times. If you allow anyone in your exhibit to talk with the press, you're asking for trouble. No matter how effectively you train your staff, the stories will never come out the same. In addition, the media appreciate having a special contact within the company. They know this person has been assigned to work with them, and they know they can contact this same person for a possible follow-up. The person assigned should know exactly what information is available to the media and what is not, and then stick to those guidelines.

Here are some media interview tips offered by Marilyn Hawkins, owner of Hawkins and Company, a Seattle-based marketing and management communications agency:

- Listen as much as you talk. Understand the reporter's questions.
- Be friendly and engaging, but neither deferential nor defensive.
- Make your key points as simply—and as often—as possible.

- Don't ramble. Make your point and stop.
- If necessary, take time and educate the reporter. But don't do it condescendingly.
- Be quotable. Think in terms of attention-getting headlines and lead paragraphs.
- Never lie or intentionally mislead.
- Don't say anything off the record, unless you possess incredible media savvy.
- Avoid defaming anyone or anything. If the interview is about someone in particular, don't get sidetracked into talking about other people and other issues, especially negatively.
- If you don't understand the reporter's question, don't try to answer it. Politely ask for clarification.
- Never give a reporter words with which to hang yourself.
- If you don't know the answer to a question, admit it. Offer to get the answer as soon as possible, and then be sure and follow up.
- Avoid at all costs the words "No comment." There are a million ways to address a tough question short of raising that red flag.
- At the conclusion of the interview, ask the reporter if he or she got everything he or she needed.
- If the story turns out well, send the reporter a brief note of acknowledgment.

Wear Your Badge Properly

Most people are right-handed, so they automatically put their name tag on the left side of their coat or blouse. At a show, you don't want to make it difficult for an attendee to read your name, but when you wear it on the left side, that's exactly what you're doing. Wear it on the right side, near the face. The reason for this is that you shake hands with the right hand. Consequently, the right shoulder leans toward the person and the left moves away. A badge worn on the right side moves toward the person being met. In addition, wearing it high makes it even easier for the attendee to read.

Keep Your Exhibit Clean

There are three things that an attendee observes immediately in every exhibit: the overall display, the personnel, and the booth's appearance. Even though you might have a service that cleans at night or comes by periodically during the day, your booth can still get cluttered and dirty. Make it a habit to inspect your booth on an ongoing basis. Empty ashtrays and trash cans; clear the area of unnecessary loose literature and other print materials; put briefcases and coats out of sight; and pick up cups and trash left behind by attendees. You might want to assign a new person during each shift to keep the booth clean. That way everybody will participate in a seemingly demeaning, but important, activity.

I have been harping on a lot of little things to pay attention to during the show, but these things make the difference between success and failure. There's a wise saying: "Winners make a habit of doing the things that losers don't like to do."

When You're Awake, You're Working

One of the biggest myths about trade shows is that they are some sort of vacation. Trade shows, no matter where they are held, are not vacations. When done correctly, they are hard work. The hours can be long. You stand on your feet all day. You meet hundreds, possibly thousands, of strangers, taking you out of your comfort zone. You eat poorly and irregularly; convention food services have never been known for gourmet cuisine. You get headaches from working your brain overtime. Your eyes burn from the lighting, not to mention the smoke in the arena. Your hand throbs from shaking other hands all day long. You're burned out from giving the same sales pitch over and over. You lose patience with the lookie-loos who just take up your time asking stupid questions, not to mention the kids under 18 who snuck in past the guards.

Trade shows are not a reward, but they can be rewarding. You can generate enough business to last you several months, maybe several years. The catch is that, at a trade show, when you're awake, you're working. There are no working hours during the week of a trade show. It's not a 10 A.M. to 6 P.M. job, after which you go out with your buddies for dinner and drinks. You have to take advantage of every opportunity to contact your customers and potential prospects. Meet a prospect for breakfast, offer one a ride to the show in your rental car, or, if you don't have one, share a taxi. At least sit next to a buyer on the bus.

When you take a break at the show, the break isn't from working, it's from standing. Take a prospect away with you for a cup of coffee. Schedule lunch with a member of the media. Arrange to meet a new customer for drinks after the show closes. And, of course, schedule dinner with someone important. Your rest period comes after dinner, in your room.

If this concept turns you off to trade shows, don't let it. It's usually only for a few days. For the amount of potential new business, you can sacrifice yourself for a few days.

Consider a Hospitality Suite

There are only two reasons to have a hospitality suite at a trade show. One is to intentionally extend the hours of the show itself. The second is to display a prototype so new you don't want to risk your competition seeing it at the show. Hospitality suites are among the most expensive and abused of trade show costs. That's why it's important to ensure its success when leasing one. A few points to keep in mind about hospitality suites follow.

Have specific objectives for the hospitality suite that are congruent with your objectives at the show. Too many companies just throw a big party. These events are too expensive and take too much planning time away from the real purpose of the trade show. Do you want to give longer and more private demonstrations of a new product to a prospect? Do you want to offer a more sedate way of displaying your products to a select few? Great! Use a hospitality suite. Do you want to impress a lot of friends, media, and enemies? Then give a party for no particular reason.

Always have a display in the suite. Why would you possibly go through the expense of having a hospitality suite, food, and refreshments without also having your product on display? Unfortunately, it happens all the time.

Set specific and reasonable hours for the suite to be open and then stick by them. The suite doesn't need to be open all night long. You'll show much more professionalism by announcing and posting that the suite is open for a specific period of time. For example, if the show ends at 6:00, have your suite open from 6:00 to 8:00 P.M. That way you dine at a reasonable hour.

Make Advance Reservations

My friend Phil Wexler, coauthor of the popular book *Non-Manipulative Selling*, passed this idea along. When you travel out of town for a show, looking for a place to eat at night gets to be a big hassle. In fact, at some of the larger shows, you might have trouble getting into restaurants at a decent hour. Advance reservations eliminate this problem.

Phil says to make reservations as far ahead as six months before the show. Book for a decent hour, such as 7:30. Then, when you ask prospects and customers to go out at night, you look like you've got connections.

If you don't know which restaurants to call, there are several references to consult. Call your hotel's concierge and ask for a list of local recommendations. *Sales and Marketing Management* magazine annually lists the top business eateries in the United States. Travel books generally list a number of good restaurants in each city. However, the best way to find where to eat is to ask someone you know who lives in that city.

Finally, be sure to make enough reservations for your staff and any possible guests. A good rule of thumb is to double the number in your staff.

Study the Competition

In *The Art of War,* Sun Tzu states,

> What enables the good general to strike and conquer, and achieve things beyond the reach of ordinary men, is foreknowledge. Now this knowledge cannot be obtained inductively from experience, nor any deductive calculation. . . . The dispositions of the enemy are ascertainable through spies and spies alone.

In today's business world, it's not enough to know your own product and understand the needs of your customer. You must also have complete knowledge of what the competition is doing. Trade shows are unique not only because buyers come to you, but because the competition is right across the aisle. It's a great opportunity for you to do some firsthand market research and information gathering. Be a spy. Take the time to walk the show thoroughly and completely.

I've already talked about having your sales staff visit the competition. Now I'll describe a little more specifically what you should be looking for while walking the show.

Part of the reason you're at the trade show is to learn as much about your competition as possible. Go ahead and be bold in approaching them. There's no law against walking into their booths and looking over their products and literature.

It's not unusual for a contingent of people to act as if they own the show. They act like the whole place is their oyster and all the information in the hall is theirs for the taking. And speaking of taking, they take pictures everywhere and of everything. Once in a while someone will walk up and ask them to stop, but not usually.

If you act like you own the place, you can get away with a lot. Get a camera and a blank note pad, and go out and gather as much information as you can. Investigate your competition. Look for differences between your products, your salespeople, your exhibits, your literature, your customer perceptions, and your preshow marketing tactics and their effect on performance. (This last one doesn't necessarily have to be done at the show, but should be considered when gathering all this information.)

Once you have put this information together, you'll want to evaluate the differences by asking these questions: Is the difference positive or negative? How big is the difference? What brought on this difference and when? How does the difference affect you in the eyes of the customers? How can you respond to the difference, and how can your competitors respond? If the advantage is in your favor, how easy would it be for the competition to eliminate it? How can you sustain the advantage? For how long? Can you continue to build on the advantage? Other than your competition, what factors could affect the advantage?

Maybe you can't take the time to go off during the show and gather this valuable information. If that's the case, try to get to the show early enough to walk through undisturbed. Often, this is the best time to do it anyway. The booths are devoid of people and everything is usually displayed for your uninterrupted viewing.

All this competitor analysis will not only help you with future trade shows, it will also give you a lot of valuable information for your marketing strategy. So, if at all possible, don't let this tremendous opportunity to gather information slip away. If you can't go deeply into it, at least keep some of these questions in mind while walking the show. At least get something!

Look at the Show in General

As you're walking around, take in the general feel of the show. Does it seem to be a fairly upbeat atmosphere? Are the exhibitors in a good mood? Are the displays new or refurbished? Are companies spending money on this particular show? How's the attendance? If the show is sponsored by an association, talk with some of the officials. Do they feel the industry is on the upswing, or is the show a downer? Are the aisles empty? Do you hear such things over the PA system as, "Buyer in Aisle 3,000! Buyer in Aisle 3,000," followed by exhibitors running to grab the guy?

Look for new ideas for exhibit design. What booth are you attracted to and why? What new ideas do you see that you might be able to use in future shows? What are the most crowded booths and what do they feature? What new trends do you see in these exhibits? Why are certain booths more crowded than others? Is it because they have *Playboy* centerfolds signing autographs, or do they have a legitimate business reason for all the activity?

Personal Trade Show Survival Kit

Here's what I recommend you be sure not to forget:

- Business cards (about five times as many as you think you need)
- Corporate letterhead, note pads, and envelopes
- Breath spray (not mints or gum)
- Ballpoint pens and markers
- Your date book or pocket calendar
- Footpads (trust me, your feet will definitely know the difference)
- Comfortable shoes (this is no place to break in new ones)
- Cellophane tape and paper clips
- Large 9 by 12 envelopes and mailing labels
- Traveler's checks and credit cards for on-site payments
- Baby powder (trust me again, each morning coat your body with it, you'll feel much fresher all day)
- Extra accessories
- Shoe polish
- Bandages
- Aspirin or aspirin-free pain reliever
- Antacids
- Sunglasses
- Pocket stapler, staples, and staple remover

CHAPTER 8

Postshow Follow-Up
Closing the Loop

The trade show closes, an immense success for your company. You were thoroughly prepared, primed, and pumped. Your booth staff, well drilled, obtained the maximum number of qualified leads. Your booth constantly drew customers and waves of new prospects. They all admired your exhibit and professionalism. Everyone returned home exhausted, but with lots of leads, feeling elated.

Now that you've just worked your tail off for a week, can you relax? You excelled in phase one, preshow planning. You did a great job on phase two, the show itself. But phase three remains: postshow follow-up and evaluation.

Those leads are hot, and your company name is fresh in their minds. *Now* is the time to act! Normally, people returning from exhibiting at a trade show get right back into the regular office routine. Don't delay: Pursue all those leads from the show immediately.

The Typical Routine

John Smith returns after working last week's MegaTron Show in Las Vegas. He's exhausted but knows there is a pile of old mail to open and dozens of phone calls that need to be returned. He dives into the mail and enthusiastically begins sorting it. A coworker stops by his office asking how the show went.

"Fantastic," says John. "We worked hard, but it was worth it. We must have walked out with more than 600 new leads!" He then relates a couple of war stories, after which the coworker leaves and John gets back to his mail and phone messages.

This routine continues for a day or two, when John finds out he needs to get going on a new sales campaign. Also, the new product catalog is late for production. Several strategy planning meetings with upper management require attendance, too. There's also the business trip to Region Three for the formal presentation to that big distributor. A nagging feeling that he has forgotten something keeps bugging John, but as the days turn into weeks, it passes.

Sound familiar? OK, so I wrote it especially to fit the needs of this book. That's literary license. The point is, I'll bet it closely reflects most situations. What's missing from John's work? The follow-up on those 600 leads! Leads from a trade show are hot, and every day that goes by cools them down a degree or two.

I have an ongoing, informal, unscientific trade show survey. I make it a habit to ask trade show attendees their impressions of a recent show. I also ask how follow-up has been with them. These are buyers I'm talking to. The results over the past few years have been disappointing, if not downright ridiculous. For example, at the time of this writing, it is several weeks after the Fall COMDEX in Las Vegas. This is a big show—several thousand exhibitors taking up over a million square feet, with more than 180,000 attendees. People take this show seriously, but apparently not the exhibitors. I've already spoken with three attendees from COMDEX, three legitimate buyers of high-tech products. They estimated that between them they stopped and requested information from more than 300 companies. But as of today, they have received only four follow-up responses from the show. That's less than a 2 percent response after five weeks! Something's wrong here. In fact, the question each of these buyers asks me is this: "If those exhibitors aren't going to bother to follow up in a timely fashion after the show, why should I even go at all?" I have to agree.

Trade show follow-up is the reason you exhibited in the first place. Getting new leads is one of the primary objectives for attending a show. Those leads must be of primary importance after the show is over.

Steve Miller's Follow-Up Philosophy

Effective Follow-Up Begins with Preshow Planning

This simple step will save you a tremendous amount of time after the show. As part of your preshow planning process, write your follow-up letter before you leave. Enter it in your word processor, leaving space for the prospect's name and address, plus room for a personalized comment—if you fill out your lead form completely, you'll have information for this section. By including one sentence that refers back to something you talked about at the trade show, the prospects won't care that they're getting a form letter. Once you get back from the show you can turn over the leads to whoever is handling follow-up.

The 48-Hour Follow-Up Rule

There seem to be two prevailing schools of thought regarding the time frame for follow-up. We've already discussed what I call the Infinity School of Follow-Up. That's the one where there is no time limit; you can follow up anytime. The second school of thought regarding follow-up is a fairly new one. It's the "Let's Spend Lots and Lots of Money and Get the Information to the Prospects Before They Even Fly Back to Their Office—Won't They Be Impressed" School. Under this system, you send your leads at the end of each day back to the office by overnight express, where they are turned into product information kits with form letters and, in turn, sent out to the prospect by overnight express. (I hope you have a big budget.)

I've got to admit, though, if I had to pick between the Infinity School and the LSLALOMAGTITTPBTEFBTTO—WTBI School, I'd pick the second one. But it's still not good enough. On the surface, it seems like a great idea, but there is a basic flaw regarding human nature that's being overlooked. After you've been out of your office for several days, what are the two things guaranteed to be waiting for you on your desk when you return? A two-foot stack of mail, and a one-foot stack of pink telephone messages. Most people just don't want to deal with these piles any longer than is absolutely necessary. As a result, they literally buzz through them, culling out the necessary from the unnecessary just to remove the desktop clutter. They just aren't going to spend much time on each piece of mail in the stack, even if it is a red, white, and blue express package. The process of culling through their mail will be quick. They'll spend only a few seconds on each piece, if that much.

Frankly, I don't want my expensive follow-up package to be in that pile. That's why I developed what I call the 48-Hour Rule. The 48-Hour Rule is a simple, effective way of reaching prospects in a timely fashion. The goal is for the follow-up package to arrive no earlier than 48 hours after the show ends, and no later than 48 hours after that. Think of it as a 48-hour "window." (*Note:* The 48-Hour Rule is based on working days; it does not include weekends or holidays.)

There are four reasons for following this plan:

Visibility.   You don't land in the big pile of mail. As I was just discussing, people spend about two days going through their mail and phone messages. Send your material so it lands on their desks after the big pile has been cleared off.

Memory.   The show is still fresh in prospects' minds. It's still only been a couple of days since they were at the show. If you developed a good rapport with them, they'll remember you and your product line.

Credibility.   You told prospects you'll be sending the information out right away, and by following this rule, you've done it. You've anchored in the prospects' minds just how professional and dependable you are.

Personal access.   It gives you a reason for a follow-up telephone call. By getting the information out in such a timely manner, you can now call the prospects to check and see if they received the information.

The 5/10/20/40 Follow-Up

Once you've sent the information off to arrive within the 48-hour window, you can personally follow up by telephone in a timely fashion. Unless you've already set up a personal appointment, this is the next best thing to being there.

Five working days after the show closes, your packet of information should be in the hands of the prospects. Give them a call and ask if they received the information they requested. Be sure and emphasize that you had promised to send it to them, and you are following up to make sure they received it.

If they have received the material, politely ask if they've had a chance to look through it. If so, ask if you could set a phone appointment with them to discuss how you might be able to work together. Don't assume that because you've got them on the line, they have time to talk with you right then. Be considerate and offer to speak with them at their convenience. If they have received the information, but haven't looked it over yet, confidently say that you'll follow up in a week to answer any questions they have. This will put the onus on them to look through the packet. If they haven't received the information yet, simply say you're sure they'll receive it in a day or two and you'll follow up again next week. Again, make sure to set the phone appointment.

The object of the 5/10/20/40 Follow-Up is that you talk with the prospect 5 working days after the show, and then 10, 20, and 40 working days after the show. By then, you should know where you stand. This is not to say that you must talk with them all four times. If you close the deal on the second call, you don't need to continue this pattern. Of course, good customer service after the sale is important, but that's another issue.

The beauty of the 5/10/20/40 Follow-Up is that in a short period of time, you know exactly where you stand. If prospects have a need and a desire, you know you'll be staying on top of them until you get the order. If, for whatever reason, you determine that they don't fit your criteria for prospects, you can stop spending your valuable time on them.

One additional objective I have in that time frame is to get the name of another possible contact from the prospects. After meeting them at the show and following up regularly, I usually build a fairly good rapport with prospects. Because of this good rapport, I can ask for referrals, whether or not we do business together. In fact, sometimes the ones I don't work with feel a sense of obligation to help me because of the time I've put into building our relationship.

Remember, the three phases of the trade show campaign are before, during, and after the show. Your goal is to use preshow marketing effectively to entice customers and prospects to visit your booth at the trade show. Then, through professional trade show selling and presenting, you bring yourself one step closer to your goals. Then, with timely and effective postshow follow-up, you tie the three parts together synergistically. You have taken what was in the past a two-, three-, four-, or five-day event, and turned it into a successful four- to five-month marketing campaign.

Measuring Success

Evaluation is widely considered to be the hardest part of trade show marketing. Actually, if you set those measurable objectives in the beginning that I discussed in Chapter 2, this is the easy part.

There is another way, however, that will help you measure the success of your trade shows easily and effectively. Essentially it is a three-step process requiring that you set quantitative goals to be measured at three different time intervals: immediately following the show, six months later, and again 12 months later. With this method, all you need to do is compare the results of your show with the original objectives.

Let's say, for example, your three objectives are:

Immediate—500 leads
six months—20 new accounts
12 months—20 additional new accounts

This means that you expect to leave the show with 500 solid leads. Then, within the next six months, you expect to turn them into 20 new accounts, and after an additional six months, you expect to acquire 20 more new accounts, directly attributable to the show.

This process is fairly simple, requiring only a customer profile form that includes information on where the lead came from. You should have that anyway. It's important you know whether your new customers come from a direct mail campaign, customer referrals, cold calls, or trade shows. Such information shows you where to focus your marketing efforts.

Some of your goals may be more difficult to measure, but you should still do your best. For example, let's say you want to create a new corporate image through an updated logo. Your exhibit is designed to focus on your new look, so your objective is to have as many people come through your booth as possible. You still want their business cards, but don't have the staff size to qualify everybody. Offer some sort of dynamite incentive to get them to leave their business cards, such as drawing for an all-expense-paid trip to Hawaii. By totaling the number of business cards you receive, you'll know how many people came through your booth. This would equal the number of impressions your new logo made. Then, after the show, do a follow-up telemarketing campaign to accomplish two things: to determine the impact your new logo made and to qualify potential prospects. This way, you're not only measuring a nebulous goal, but getting some solid leads as well.

While your objectives for a show may not be one of these, it is important that you do have some objectives on paper for postshow evaluation. Too many companies never evaluate their trade shows and that's a mistake. Just like any other strategy in your marketing mix, you need to measure the success or failure of each risk.

The Decision to Return

Most companies automatically sign up for a show after it appears that the show was worthwhile. Considering that most companies don't even measure the success or failure of a show, other than by gut feeling, this can be a real mistake.

Every time you consider going to a show, even if you've been going for years, you must make sure that show is right for you. Companies change, trends change, industries change, markets change, and trade shows change. When you consider returning to a show, reread Chapter 2 and use the selection guidelines. Then go to four other sources for more feedback.

Customers

Ask them whether they believe the show is still one your company should attend. They'll be straight with you. Something may have changed in the show over the years so your customers no longer feel that the show has value for you.

Staff

These people work the show floor. They should know whether or not the show still works for your company.

Competition

Your competition is a valuable source of information. If the trade show is moving away from your original objectives, it's probably moving away from those of your competitors, too. If you've got a good relationship with them, ask their opinion.

Trade Journals

Trade journals know what's happening in the industry. If a trade show is in trouble or is changing markets, the journals should know about it. They can give you their opinion on exhibiting in the show.

Trade shows are expensive and time-consuming. Don't just arbitrarily make a decision to go to a show because you think it's right. Be ruthless in your determination to make an intelligent decision. After all, it's your money and your time.

Stay Sharp!

Although the trade show industry is very large, with estimates placed as high as $65 billion spent annually on exhibitions, I believe we are now approaching a crossroads. Innovations for more effective marketing are developed every day. Corporations are becoming more sophisticated in their techniques and more demanding of their results. Trade shows need to produce results, not just offer an exercise in exposure.

New trends and developments in computers, audiovisual presentations, sales techniques, communications, and lead tracking are certainly making trade shows more efficient and effective. They also enhance the value of trade shows, making them more and more important.

Don't get lost in the crowd by staying in the same old rut of trade show participation. Use the methods and techniques described in this book, and then be on the lookout for other new tools you can use. Have you incorporated database management software to compile and track leads generated at shows? Have you joined the information superhighway through on-line communications with your salespeople, customers, and prospects? Is your E-mail address printed on your business cards? Have you looked into the new capabilities offered by exhibit houses, as far as lightweight construction, modular design, CAD renderings, and new photographic processes? Have you incorporated multimedia into your exhibit presentations? Have you set your exhibit up for communicating with all attendees, including those from other countries? Do you think Virtual Reality will be the end of trade shows? (It won't.) Do you carry a laptop computer to the show, so you can input all your new leads, and then download them directly to the home office by modem?

To be sure, the trade show industry will continue to evolve and grow into the new century. Technology will affect it greatly, but technology won't make trade shows go away. As John Naisbitt said in *MegaTrends*, "The more high-tech we become, the more high-touch we'll need." Trade shows will continue to provide that opportunity to reach out and touch someone.

Trade shows are expensive. It takes a lot of time to do them right. But, if you invest that money and time wisely and aggressively, you can turn trade shows into your most effective and most profitable marketing tool.

Where to Get More Information

Here are a number of different sources you may want to contact for further information:

Center for Exhibition Industry Research
4350 East West Highway
Suite 401
Bethesda, MD 20814
301/907-7626
www.ceir.org

Computer Event Marketing Association
490 Boston Post Road
Sudbury, MA 01776-3301
978/443-3330
www.cemaonline.com

Exhibit Designers and Producers Association
5775 G Peachtree Dunwoody Road
Suite 500
Atlanta, GA 30342
404/303-7310
www.edpa.com

Exhibit Surveys
7 Hendrickson Avenue
Red Bank, NJ 07701
732/741-3170

Exposition Service Contractors Association
400 S. Houston Street
Suite 210
Dallas, TX 75202
214/742-9217

Healthcare Convention and Exhibitors Association
5775 G Peachtree Dunwoody Road
Suite 500
Atlanta, GA 30342
404/303-7310
www.hcea.org

International Association of Convention and Visitors Bureaus
2000 L Street NW
Suite 702
Washington, DC 20036
202/296-7888
www.iacvb.org

International Association for Exposition Management
5001 LBJ Freeway
Suite 350
Dallas, TX 75244
972/458-8002
www.iaem.org

Trade Show Bureau
(see Center for Exhibition Industry Research)

Trade Show Exhibitors Association (formerly International Exhibitors Association)
5501 Backlick Road
Suite 105
Springfield, VA 22151
703/941-3725
www.tsea.org

Publications

Exhibitor
206 S. Broadway
Suite 745
Rochester, MN 55904
507/289-6556
www.exhibitornet.com

Exhibit Builder
22900 Ventura Boulevard
Suite 245
Woodland Hills, CA 91364
800/356-4451

Successful Meetings
355 Park Avenue South
New York, NY 10010
212/592-6200
www.successmtgs.com

Tradeshow Week Publications
5700 Wilshire Boulevard
Suite 120
Los Angeles, CA 90036
323/965-5300
www.tradeshowweek.com

On-line Industry Links

Expobase
www.expobase.com

Expoguide
www.expoguide.com

Trade Show Central
www.tscentral.com

University of Nevada at Las Vegas
www.unlv.edu

Trade Show News Network
www.tsnn.com

Index

About the Author

Steve Miller is an independent marketing consultant specializing in the trade show industry. His innovative, results-driven exhibit marketing techniques have been written about in more than 200 trade journals and newspapers, including *Fortune, Sales & Marketing Management, Success* magazine, the AMA's *Small Business Reports, Business Marketing, Washington CEO, Medical Industry Executive, Exhibitor Magazine,* and *Expo*. Steve's corporate clients have documented millions of dollars in revenues through the unique methods he's developed. An in-demand consultant and trainer, he has presented over 1,000 speeches, seminars, and workshops around the world, and works with such organizations as Coca-Cola, Boeing Commercial Airplane, Halliburton, Sara Lee, Philips Electronics, the Food Marketing Institute, and the National Association of Broadcasters.

Steve lives in Federal Way, Washington, with his best friends, Kay and Kelly—his wife and daughter.

For information about Steve's consulting, speaking, training, and audio/video educational systems:

The Adventure of Trade Shows
32706 - 39th Avenue SW
Federal Way, WA 98023
253/874-9665
Fax 253/874-9666
E-mail txrdshwstev@aol.com
www.theadventure.com

162